J. Luxton

*Winners never quit.
And quitters never win!*

Vince Lombardi

Julia is no quitter…

The stroke at 32 while pregnant gave her determination to get through it to give life to her baby.

Years of rehabilitation followed enabling her to drive again and return to teaching and take a degree. Her physiotherapy is an ongoing treatment to keep her right side active and her compensation from it all has been her children who are so proud of her.

BE INSPIRED…
BE VERY INSPIRED.

SUNSHINE FROM THE SHADOWS

Dedication

To Mum, my rock, for just being there.

To Laura-Jo, my daughter, and my best friend.

To Perryn, who, like me, overcame all the odds and is lucky to be here.

In Memoriam: Aunty Muriel, Uncle Bill and Grandpa Joe, without whom none of this would be possible.

And always remembered – Lynn Green (nee Laity). Everlasting love.

Julia Luxton B.A.

SUNSHINE FROM THE SHADOWS

Vanguard Press

VANGUARD PAPERBACK

© Copyright 2010
Julia Luxton B.A.

The right of Julia Luxton B.A. to be identified as author of
this work has been asserted by her in accordance with the
Copyright, Designs and Patents Act 1988.

All Rights Reserved

No reproduction, copy or transmission of this publication
may be made without written permission.
No paragraph of this publication may be reproduced,
copied or transmitted save with the written permission of the publisher,
or in accordance with the provisions
of the Copyright Act 1956 (as amended).

Any person who commits any unauthorised act in relation to
this publication may be liable to criminal
prosecution and civil claims for damages.

A CIP catalogue record for this title is
available from the British Library.

ISBN 978 1 84386 622 0

Vanguard Press is an imprint of
Pegasus Elliot MacKenzie Publishers Ltd.
www.pegasuspublishers.com

First Published in 2010

Vanguard Press
Sheraton House Castle Park
Cambridge England

Printed & Bound in Great Britain

Acknowledgements

Thanks to all the physiotherapists who have treated me over the years, who are more intimate with my left side than I am! Especially those at Marie Therese House in Hayle. I remember too that nurse – all those years ago – who told me to always look for someone worse off than yourself when you're feeling down – a good lesson for us all to learn.

I thank Paul Triggs and the Kernewek singers who helped me find my voice again. Laura, for keeping me on the straight and narrow. And Judi, for trying to tempt me otherwise; for all those cups of coffee and the encouragement.

PROLOGUE

This is the story about my life... that is rather mundane, and the events that have gone on around me that shaped it.

All the tales from the 'Tin Tabernacle' are in here including the war stories, how my parents met and the Torrey Canyon oil disaster of 1967. I was thirteen at the time and I remember watching my father sinking deep into the oil and it spilling over the top of his boots as he waded out to rescue an injured bird.

In here, is how the disaster brought in a great number of army lads who suffered badly from the effects of the detergent that was used to disperse the oil, which made them cry with pain as it burned their eyes and how romance blossomed from such suffering.

Also how my mother asked permission, from the farmer where my dad worked, to use our cottage as a Bed and Breakfast property although it had no bathroom and a loo that was at the end of a very long garden They worked hard so that they would have enough money to send me on a school cruise and later on to college,

And how we welcomed celebrities into our house and made firm friendships for life, especially two lads from Hull who broke into the folk scene in the 1970s and taught me how to sing and play the guitar.

It's all about my village life in the '60s, '70s and the '80s, when all we had was a shop, a post office, a pub, a church and a chapel; and the arguing between the church wardens about where the best place to worship was.

How the 'Boat cove boys', Pebble Eye, Percy, Willy Bray and 'Our Boy Jack' all gathered on their bench daily overlooking the sea, telling stories of how things used to be and frightening trippers with their stories of wrecks, ghosts and people 'walking abroad' at all hours.

My Grandpa Joe, although he left school at the age of thirteen, was the most educated man in the village, no taller than a 'hob', he looked the size of an ant as he led a team of shire horses ploughing the fields on the land that he took great pride in.

He had his own unique personality and many tales to tell, especially declaring proudly about his physical abilities in the place where he climbed a ladder for the first time when descending down into the mine. And another time when he was putting mangles in the field, taking them off the cart with a pike and when the horse didn't go fast enough, Grandpa Joe prodded the horse with the end of the pike making the horse rear up, throwing him in between the shaft and the cart. The horse then ran over him breaking some of his ribs. The quickest way to transport him to his home was to unhinge the nearest gate. He had no money to spend on doctors' treatment so he lay on a board in the front room for weeks until he was well enough to move about again.

Then came the disasters: when my dad caught his hand in the milling machine and lost two fingers and the top of his thumb. The compensation of £200 pounds we spent on our first car. His life came to an end unexpectedly in 1992, when on an OAP coach trip to Nottingham, he had suffered a heart attack and was taken to the Birmingham General Hospital. His deformity confirmed the identification that it was my dad.

Then my own life… 1976 I started teaching at Pendeen, near St Just, the furthest school on the south-west coastline. Many of the pupils' fathers worked down the Geevor mine until the disaster happened. I got married in 1978 in Perranuthnoe Church and kept my eye on the church entrance from my bedroom window until my groom went in.

After I was married I moved to Heamoor and carried on teaching at Pendeen. In 1982 I had my first child, Laura-Jo. Maybe it had something to do with getting married on 1 April. I should have heard the warning bells when 'F' said: 'Well if we've got to do it, it might as well be ALL FOOLS DAY.'

It was also The Grand National Day, so when I came out of the church everyone had gone off to the reception to watch the racing. Later my new husband cheated on me continuously and like many I was the last to know. The only good thing that came out of that marriage was that we had Laura in 1982, and she has been my rock ever since.

But in 1985 all my dreams got shattered while I was pregnant with my second child, when I suffered a major stroke. Luckily the baby Perryn, a boy, survived but I completely lost the use of my left side.

I returned to teaching at a later date and got a degree while my own children were studying. So we all ended up celebrating together and I proved to everyone, I wasn't as thick as I looked.

Being a stroke survivor of some twenty years, two of the main things that have kept me going during this time have been the love and support of my family and the near obsession inside me to *think positive* in any given situation when things have been difficult. Today I live on the realisation that I am lucky to be alive although my life has changed considerably over the years. I had a migraine stroke when I was just 32 caused by immense stress. At the time I was a full-time teacher loving my job and playing the guitar and singing for pleasure.

I always had migraines but when this one lasted from Friday to Tuesday without easing up, I began to think that something was seriously wrong. The proof came when my mouth felt as if it was no longer connected to my brain and all my words were tangled up inside my head. They could not escape, and even my hand refused to write down anything at all.

My family call me 'Jackie Sunshine' simply because I am always smiling!

So there is always:

'Sunshine from the Shadows'

Chapter One
THE JOKE'S ON ME

There is one thing I can swear to... and that is... I was not an APRIL FOOL BABY...

Honestly! My mum claims that she kept her legs crossed until after midnight on April 1st 1954 so that I didn't enter the world until 12.45am on April 2nd.

The custom in those days was to have your babies at home with only the midwife present, so who is to say at what time exactly I was born. There I was this tiny newborn with a head full of ginger hair... odd... as none of the rest of the family were!

My brother Roger who was ten years older bore a mop of sleek fair hair that looked almost white, and my sister who was seven years older was naturally dark and appertaining to black on a good day.

So as we ruled out the butcher, the baker and the coalman, it was wondered aloud in the family ranks as to whose little girl I was. This was all a joke of course, but we couldn't help wondering among ourselves if we were in fact all fathered by the same man. My father would have been aghast if he knew about such rumours, so we all concluded that we were celebration babies anyway: my brother in 1945 was an obvious celebration of the ending of the war and in 1947 perhaps my sister was the result of the end of some kind of rationing.

Likewise, if I was conceived in the summer of 1953, it was a well known fact that the nation was in the throes of celebrating the new queen's coronation in the early fifties, so we all maintained having a joyous start in life.

Then there was the naming of this new baby.

My sister was named after my Aunty Muriel, who lived in Cornwall. There were a few rumblings that my dad had a great aunt called Julia and so this was suggested for me. But there was little enthusiasm shown for this newest member of the family... words such as 'mistake' came forward when my parents were acknowledged and questioned about their three children. It was a word I had heard many times while I was growing up, so I grew up in the knowledge that perhaps, unlike the wise family planning of today, my appearance in the family wasn't greeted with as much fervour as that of my brother or sister.

Later I was to learn that my father's sacrifice, on being told that there would be one more addition to the family, was to give up smoking, so that the money could be stretched just that little further. This he did instantly, replacing the packet of 'Woodbines' in his pocket for the ubiquitous bag of boiled sweets which he offered generously to all in exchange for stories and the like.

My father cycled to Great Torrington a few days after my birth to register his new daughter and, as no one had questioned his suggestions, I was called Julia after Grandma Ursula's sister and Marion after yet another family member that he liked.

My home was in Little Torrington at No 4 Yarde Cottages, and yes, this place sounded as dull as it really was. The cottages were situated beside the railway line that transported the china clay from North Devon down to the

South. They were haphazardly thrown together and propped each other up, as if they were glued together by the continuous layer of sticky soot, deposited from the trains on their journeys – the station being just a few yards from the houses.

Baby Julia in her mother's arms

Dumping Hill, Shebbear

My mum could master most things in her life at Yarde but with two young babies and all that washing, even she gave up when it came to the ironing. She had an iron that had a middle section that was heated in the fire then put in an iron frame – then the whole thing was physically thumped down on the washing to produce the required effect.

This was one thing that mum just could not handle, but when she learned that Grandpa Luxton had an electric iron at Dumping Hill, then the problem was sorted; so with the ironing loaded on the bottom of the coach pram and one child at each end, she would set off on the five-mile journey to Shebbear.

Dumping Hill was a foreboding house set on the hill just outside the village. Its structure was more akin to the mansions of a Gothic novel but its occupants were as friendly as any in-laws might be to their son's new wife.

It was Grandpa Isaac who was the most welcoming. With his soft gentle features and mild manner it was difficult to picture him as a special constable in the Devon constabulary. But unfortunately due to an accident where he fell off his bike and sustained head injuries, he became prone to bad headaches which seeped all his energy leaving him good for nothing.

But most of the time he was just the peaceful underlying kingpin to sustaining the unity of his family, which consisted of three girls and two boys, their first born having died at birth.

Grandma Ursula was just the opposite of him; she was a small, frail looking woman, moody, tiresome and always finding fault with Isaac who would bend over backwards to please her, although whatever he did was never enough. She would sit in her chair bent over the stove trying to keep warm and calling for his attention: saying 'Isaac where's my tea?' 'Where's my slippers?' And Isaac would immediately come running to her commands.

The only time they seemed happy was on a Saturday night when all the family would meet up for a shindig. The huge table in the parlour would be crammed with food for when the family came back from the pub. The drinking and carousing would carry on until the early hours of the next morning.

We were the children of the various marriages and we were all included in such partying – if not for very long. As the food disappeared from the table and the crumbs wiped away, Uncle Albert who was Aunty Betty's husband, would get a bit jolly; he would start off playing the spoons which was quite an art, but this would progress to his dancing on the table.

It was at about this stage in the proceedings that we kids were ushered off to bed. I have vague memories of long corridors leading to the bedroom where we were all deposited in a big iron-framed bed with a very warm goose cover.

It was a relief to finally get to the bedroom because the journey upstairs meant that we had to pass the animals in the alcoves displayed behind glass covers. There was a particularly savage fox that had his mouth open, displaying rows of sharp teeth, and an owl, with soft downy feathers whose beady eyes followed you right up the stairs.

Once in bed there was a lot of fun to be had; we would jump up and down as we shrieked and shouted and then imagined all sorts of people were in our room. But eventually the giggling got replaced by sounds of snoring as one by one we settled down and went to sleep.

In the morning it was a different scene altogether; downstairs would be swept clean and everything would be put back in place, showing no signs that a rowdy event had ever taken place the night before.

Grandma would already have the roast cooking for the Sunday lunch and Grandpa Isaac would inevitably be found out in the vegetable patch tending to his plants.

The roast would always be delicious, followed by Grandma's rhubarb tart and custard, which I still adore. Not a favourite of my mum's though; maybe she has a deep seated dislike to it because of all those early days she spent in Devon.

The neighbours reflected this grimy existence; struggling to survive in forbidding circumstances, grimy, skinny kids whose mothers couldn't be bothered to slouch to the water pump at the end of the row to carry the water back for a decent wash; better to let their husbands rinse off their dirt at the end of their shift, than bringing it home with them.

My dad was an engine driver on the trains and found it boring, monotonous and having no future. He worked long hours to put the food on our table, but with all his good intentions we were always short of money. He met my mum during the war when he was stationed at Falmouth; it was a whirlwind romance and she had unquestionably followed him back to Devon because of his job which was now working in the clay works.

Soon after their marriage the announcement came that a baby was on the way, and although all her pre-natal checks were planned for Penzance hospital, she had little choice but to give birth to Roger in our Perranuthnoe cottage. He was apparently the first baby to be born there for a hundred years.

'Typical' making history from the moment he arrived. After the birth mum went back to Devon, coming from just a tiny Cornish village where everybody knew and helped each other, she was transported to a cold, alien land where she knew no one and had to depend on the in-laws for company and this little new soul to look after.

Roger was a very small baby weighing just five pounds. Because of the cold winter mum placed him in a drawer to sleep because this was the warmest and most comfortable place for him. As the weather improved so did his health and by the spring of 1946 he was declared fit and healthy.

From upstairs in the attic of No 4 Yarde Cottages it was possible to see Dartmoor on a clear day. It was also noted that in the very cold winter of 1947 the snow on these hills never melted all summer.

Yet through all these trying times my mother took great pride in all she did, and would never be seen in her apron at the end of the day; she would always be neatly dressed making sure she was presentable by the time dad returned home from work.

One of the things she took great pride in was the washing, especially my brother's terry towelling nappies. All were washed by hand and hung out on the line in a neat dazzling white row, only to find that during the hard winter of '47 by the time the last one was pegged firmly down, the first one was frozen stiff, so nothing actually dried; it just all froze in a block of ice.

Not only was it freezing outside, it was so cold inside that the water jug, hand-basin and window in the bedrooms were frozen for weeks. Through all this my mother's insistence on presenting an acceptable home for her family, earned her the dubious title of being called 'the duchess' of Yarde Cottages, which always reflected her aloofness from those around her.

Although the arrival of my brother was a happy occasion, it was tinged with sadness. My mum's mother was suddenly taken seriously ill with pernicious anaemia, which might today be seen as a form of leukaemia – being a lack of red blood cells. Her self-made remedy of eating raw liver in a sandwich was not affective this time.

Roger was only six weeks old at the time when mum travelled down to West Cornwall Hospital to show her, her new grandson. Unfortunately, on her arrival, she was told she could not take him into the ward. But the matron was very understanding and arranged it so that mum could stand at the window to show him to her. Sadly after the visit, Florence Thomas passed away aged just forty-eight.

My mother left Cornwall afterwards feeling even more distressed on having to go back to North Devon where we were about to experience the coldest winter on record.

Meanwhile back in Perranuthnoe, my grandfather knew how hard things were for his eldest daughter and sent her 10 shillings a week (fifty pence in today's money), which was gratefully received in the days when child benefit was just being debated in government.

My mum had also left her younger sister home at Perran. Their lives were quite similar; she also had married her wartime sweetheart, my Uncle Bill, and they had had a son too.

Theirs was the kind of love affair you only read about in books. As soon as Muriel spied Billy amongst the group of soldiers who had been invited to the Tin Tabernacle for the dance, it was said to have been a case of love at first sight. Although the village hall with its tin roof was not the most romantic place where one might meet the love of your life.

Indeed, when it rained, the water thundered down from above and it was difficult to make yourself heard above the elements. Perhaps it was just the tension in the air at the time, that we were actually at war, and the fact that enemy planes had been spotted flying low over Mounts Bay and firing in the fields over Perranuthnoe, that made everyone nervous which added urgency to the situation, but village life still went on.

My Aunty Muriel was reputed to be shy and retiring and Uncle Bill had much the same personality, the latter being quite content to just listen to the Glen Miller music and sing along rather than ask these girls to dance.

The girls who were there knew these lads had been specially invited to come, and had been chosen because of their good records with the army; being teetotallers, smart and not the type to get into a fight, it was all down to fate.

Many of the resident men had left the village to partake in the war effort, so the village was bereft of men, except for the farmworkers, so the local landowner, whose house had been commissioned by the army for its use, thought that it was time to put some sparkle into these war days, so had organised the dance and requested their company that night.

When Billy saw that the girls were pairing off with his mates he knew it was time to make a move. Muriel was still free, so, taking his courage in both hands he asked her to dance.

As they began talking Bill told her that he was from a place called Kings Norton near Birmingham and his parents worked for the Cadbury-Bournville Chocolate factory near there.

Murial told him that she was just a land girl from the next village and soon a relationship was formed. When the dance was over it was the polite thing to do to walk your partner home, so Aunty Muriel and Bill met up with my parents and contemplated walking the two miles to Perranuthnoe.

Of course there were no streetlights at this time so the winding, narrow country lane was quite a challenge. They sang and chatted in the dark until they all heard a frightful low moo, as if the cow was moaning. This put the fear of God into these town boys who had only just got used to seeing and hearing these animals in the daytime.

At night it was just too much for them so they grabbed their respective partners and ran as fast as they could all the way to the security of the village.

When they did stop for breath the girls were laughing as they explained to the men that the grim noises coming from behind the hedges were only the lamenting sounds of the female cows, because their calves had been taken from them for the night.

No stray souls were in the fields trying to frighten them – it was just normal country life. But worse was yet to come.

After saying their farewells to the girls the men had to return to their headquarters. The directions they got were to follow the main road from the hall. But after an hour and realising they were lost, they had no option but to knock on someone's door; the one they choose was Grandpa Joe's. Although these first impressions of their daughter's future husband were not the best introduction for the parents-to-be, the situation did improve and Bill was quickly accepted as

Muriel's suitor, which led to their wedding in Perranuthnoe church in June 1945.

Two years later in 1947 mum had her second baby, my sister Carolyn, and named her after my Cornish aunt; it certainly reflected my Mother's sadness and aching to come home once again.

Unlike her brother, Carolyn turned out to be a poor tempered baby and always seemed to be crying for no reason.

The couple that lived next door to us were Mr and Mrs Diamond, known affectionately as Big Di Di and little Di Di. The latter was deaf as a post and wore a squeaky rattling contraption on her chest helping her to hear, which she continually altered all the time in the attempt to get the best reception from her audience. It was as primitive as a Victorian listening horn that was used years before; it rattled and wheezed all the time as she altered the volume accordingly, by which time she had missed most of the conversation anyway.

Maybe it was through being childless that they took to Carolyn and loved her as if she was their own, but they also spoilt her by continually buying her presents causing a bone of contention with my parents, who saw this as some sort of failure on their side on not being able to have a child of their own. It caused a lot of tension between the two houses.

There was more to come as whenever arguments started in our house, Carolyn would run out and hide with these neighbours and often had to be retrieved from under their kitchen table to be taken home.

The joke's on me… the MISTAKE… Tainted for life.

But we all survived these early days in Devon, and lived to tell the tale. Then soon after my birth, a vacancy came up on the farm where Grandpa Joe worked and he recommended my father, so here was the opportunity my mum was waiting for. At last she could return to her homeland.

My Uncle and Aunt moved just up the road and the farm cottage was made available for us. So when I was just eighteen months old we took up residency in Perranuthnoe village. It came at the right time with all the stress in Devon. My untimely appearance and my sister's actions nearly had driven them to the brink of divorcing, if indeed such behaviour would have been allowed. We will never know.

Chapter Two
COMING TO PERRANUTHNOE

MAP OF THE VILLAGE OF PERRANUTHNOE 1950s - 1960s

Jackie Sunshine

I emerged from my Aunty Muriel and Uncle Bill's bathroom, all covered in talc and perfumed.

'Phew! What's that smell?' Uncle Bill joked as always.

I loved my bath sessions at their place, yet they would treat the whole thing as a big joke when they heard me coming down the stairs.

Uncle Bill would ruffle my hair and ask me if I'd clogged up the drains again. I would pretend to ignore him while giving him a toothy grin.

'See you tomorrow,' I'd call on the way out.

'If we're that unlucky, "Jackie Sunshine",' came the reply, as I went out the door and trotted home to our cosy cottage without the luxury of a bathroom.

The name "Jackie Sunshine" was started by Uncle Bill; he always said it was because I was always smiling. He related it to some song he knew about being happy and the skies being blue. I always knew that they were happy because they never spoke in loud voices like my parents did. Sometimes I even wished I might go and live with them thinking it would be a peaceful existence.

I picture myself in those early days at Perran; my hair was a ginger, blondy shade, which my mum insisted was like the colour of new copper and has kept a sample of it to this day.

It was curly too and I hated it, plus I had a face full of freckles with a line of them down my nose, which my mum called three in a row and just one on the side which was called a bonus mark.

Uncle Bill had nicknames for most of the people in the village. I knew them all and found it made me laugh whenever I saw them.

Our next-door neighbour Edgar... he was called 'Rubber Neck' because to Uncle Bill he was very nosy, and his neck bounced around in all directions to see what was happening and sure enough if there was any new gossip waiting to be spread... Edgar could do it.

I remember being so amazed by this, that if I encountered Edgar on the farm, I would unconsciously find myself staring at his neck to discover for myself if it was in fact real or rubber. It was not until I saw the presence of his Adam's apple bobbing up and down as he spoke that I knew for sure that Uncle Bill was joking.

He called my mum and her sister 'Hustle' and 'Bustle', because between them they were always on the move doing something, if not for themselves then for others in the village. My mum was also more affectionately known as 'Suee', being an abbreviation of Sylvia.

All the children of the different marriages played together. Besides my brother Roger, my playmates were Paul and John, Lyn Laity who lived at the farm, and Elizabeth Perfect her neighbour. Together we found lots to occupy us in the village.

Our favourite pastime was to wander up through the big backyard that linked John and Elizabeth's houses, each choosing a big dividing wall that separated the three houses.

John had precedence over his own backyard and chose the biggest one. Lyn and I chose the Stevens' two walls at the end of the property, walls that faced each other, so that we might watch each other's expressions when playing, and

Elizabeth was left with the enclosing wall at the end of the yard.

Once all walls had been mounted, we imagined these were our fine horses… we would pretend to gallop and trot away on exciting adventures from the security of the yard.

John was usually the 'Lone Ranger' on his horse 'Silver' and then there was the Red Indian 'Tonto' who was played in many different versions; sometimes John was the prince rescuing his fair maiden from distress. Sometimes two of us were cowboys and two were Indians and we were chasing each other, all dressed up in cowboy hats, with bits of rope for lassos or pretending to crack a fine whip.

When bored or too hot from these activities we would venture off down to Jimmy Williams' shop to spend our pocket money on penny dips, Sherbet Fountains or liquorice bits. Visiting this shop was an adventure in itself; we would try very hard to sneak in through a tiny gap in the door so that the bell wasn't forced to ring, but of course this was an impossible task. So every time the bell would give out its 'ping' sound, Mr Williams would magically appear on the other side of the counter before we even had time to cross the wide black and white checked floor to get to the sweets.

The girls and I would probably settle on a lucky dip, just to see who had the best prize in the packet, but John liked the black jacks and gob-stoppers, perhaps thinking that this added to his superiority among our ranks.

Along the counter was set out many fine delicacies which tempted every palate – huge chunks of cheese that would be cut off to order, mounds of ham, tongue and corned beef, all to be sold in the exact number of slices the customer required; and this shopkeeper had such a knack in slicing these various items that he could deftly produce a quarter of cheese or half a pound of ham to the exact amount.

There were also bags of potatoes and vegetables on the floor so that you could select the nicest produce at will.

Lyn and I also liked to play in her farmhouse. Her bedroom had another tiny room along side it and this we designated as our special place where she kept a tape recorder. Here we listened to our favourite story of 'Sparky's Magic Piano', where the piano would come to life on its own accord and play by itself. Sparky, the little boy, went along with this, pretending it was him who was playing, but of course in the end he had to admit it was the piano and not him.

We were allowed to play up by the barns at the back of the farm, and we were able to acquire a chicken's shed for a den to decorate ourselves.

Uncle Bill & Aunty Muriel

Posh shed? No! It's a Chicken's House

The fashion at the moment is to make sure you own that much-sought-after accessory to your house, the garden shed or conservatory and the more elaborate the better!

We've seen pictures of sheds in trees, revolving sheds, sheds with indoor barbecues and sheds revealing fine furniture within, at a cost of thousands of pounds, enough money in fact to buy a small flat just a few years ago.

In my youth my best friend was the daughter of the local farmer whom my dad worked for. Therefore when we were looking for somewhere special to play and away from the boys, we spied a disused chicken shed behind the farm. So one Monday morning when the men were in the barn having their elevenses, we decided to take advantage of their happy mood and laughter.

Lyn approached her father and enquired if they were using the chickens' house behind the barn? When the answer was that the chickens had been moved closer to the farmhouse because of a marauding fox, we thought we might stand a good chance.

'Oh that old thing... it's crawling,' cried her dad.

'Ugh! That's an end to that then,' we answered sadly.

Nevertheless we decided to visit it and have a look inside; it was the ideal location for us behind the barn, set up in a high position, surrounded by trees overlooking the farm and the other fields.

The door was a bit stiff and creaked as we opened it, but the smell inside was atrocious and it was full of feathers that covered the floor. A floor of chicken droppings, it had rungs across the middle and an extra bit on the end where the chickens laid their eggs. I loved visiting the shed early in the morning to open up the hatches and collect the newly laid eggs in my basket, but had never looked inside before; it was exactly what we wanted.

We both knew it would be a really hard job to clean it up, yet from our ten-year-old eyes it seemed bristling with opportunities. After all the boys didn't have anything like a den to live or hide in and we could have this as our secret hideaway.

Lynn and I went back to her father and asked what we would need to clean the chickens' house up.

'Well it will need to be thoroughly disinfected inside, two or three times and creosoted outside. It will take you most of your summer holidays,' he told us.

But we didn't care, we thought we would be one up on the boys and it would be our special secret place.

After the men had taken down the perching boughs that were positioned across the width of the chickens' house, we were set for a clean sweep. We raided our mums' cupboards for bleach, disinfectant, scrubbing brushes and bowls, then with warm water from the dairy tap we set off out on our adventure.

The smell was the worst thing to overcome; it was sharp and acrid and made our eyes sting and weep. Then there were the fleas.

First we brushed all the loose things on the floor out the door. Then we brushed the sides down and the roof.

We were covered in filth and decided we should change into our oldest clothes and put hats on to cover our heads.

We propped the door and nest boxes open so that we would get a bit of air through. We mixed the bleach in the buckets and just swamped the floor before brushing the whole lot out.

After a few times we could actually see the colour of the floor coming through underneath all that mess. We started to scrub, kneeling on old sacking we found in the Dutch barn and started from the far end towards the door. Once wasn't enough and we lost count of the number of times we attempted this gigantic task.

Our whole bodies ached and we scrubbed our knuckles raw. It was that bad that we had to leave the action for a few days. In our absence the sun came out to help the drying process.

Meanwhile we gathered together all the special things we would need to make this place seem like a second home. Lynn lived in a big farmhouse and she had a whole room next to her bedroom set aside for her bits and pieces. We knew we would want something to sit on, so we found one smallish chair, said to be a nursing chair from the past, and a 'Bunkie', that you put your feet up on when you sit in an ordinary chair. These seemed fine.

Also in the spare room we found some discarded rugs, some rolls of wallpaper, and a length of cotton material that was no longer required. In our young eyes we imagined transforming our now clean chickens' house into some kind of furnished palace and so set off down to the farm with our newly acquired decorations to make this shack our home.

On opening the door the whole place smelt so much better, but we couldn't open the small windows that were along the top of the shack because they had wire across them.

So we went in search of wire cutters from the farm's toolbox. It was a hard job trying to cut the tough wire, but eventually we did it. Cleaning the windows turned out to be an impossible task, so we thought the next best thing was to make curtains for them, to cover the grime. We brought our child's sewing machine across from the house and finished the task in no time.

We placed the rugs over the floor and immediately the place seemed much warmer and friendlier. We tried to paper the walls, but it wouldn't stick so we traipsed back to the farm to see if we could find any spare paint lying around anywhere. Luckily we found some white matt emulsion and brushes.

Day after day we brought something new to our chicken house: one good chair, even a wind up gramophone and some 78s and LPs to listen to. Tunes like, 'The Laughing Policeman', which eventually drove us a bit crazy, 'Pirates of Penzance' and Lonnie Donegan's, 'My Old Man's a Dustman'. We loved that one, especially the bit where it goes: 'Hey where's my tiger's head?' We would shout out in response: 'Five foot from his tail.'

We brought our *Famous Five* and *Secret Seven* books in and made a shelf for them at one end; perhaps we thought we were living out some of Enid Blyton's adventures.

We didn't have to lock up our shed in any way when we left it each time. In those days in our village you could leave your whole house unlocked while you went shopping, or to the beach, and it would be quite safe.

Those certainly were the days – we never moaned that we were 'bored' or had nothing to do; we would always find something to amuse ourselves with.

How lucky we were to live in the 1960s and have such fun.

John's brother Paul, being the same age as Roger, didn't often stay and play with us; they would go off playing by themselves usually ending up down at Boat cove trying to catch mullets in the rock pools, using tough cotton and a bent pin with limpets they had scraped off the rock pools for bait.

They also had a canoe of their own that they would tantalisingly skim along the still waters of Perran beach in the summer, inviting friends to swim alongside then dart off in the opposite direction.

Their showing off did lead to their downfall however, as one day the canoe, together with Roger and Paul, sank, and all that was left of them was a row of bubbles… until they marched up the sands onto the shore… carrying the ill-fated canoe on their heads.

The beach was our favourite retreat. In the days before the trippers invaded our territory, we were the only ones there.

As the Sea Gives so it Takes

My brother loved the water and always believed that the sea was in his blood. He just had to be on it, or near it, fishing from its rocks or out in his canoe. But he never learnt to swim and never wanted to. Some time later he got his own boat and then transferred to long haul trips on big shell tankers, so if he did fall overboard then only luck would get him back to shore. These super tankers were half a mile in length, so one thing he did learn was to ride a bike so he could get from one end to the other.

After the incident with his canoe and his struggle back to shore, Roger realised that one end of the beach had a rip current to it that sucked the sand literally from under your feet as you tried to wade deeper into the water. One minute the sea was gently swirling around your ankles, then your knees, but without any warning it was suddenly pulling at your chest imprisoning you in its clutches.

That was on the right hand side of the beach; the area to the left was a different matter completely. We knew that if we went right over to the rocks at the far side there was a little secluded retreat naturally carved into the cliff, which we called our own cove.

It was completely hidden from the main beach but had an opening where we could still see who was approaching; this was just the best place possible for us to have our yearly barbecues.

Message in a Bottle

It all started as an ordinary day. Lyn and I were walking along the beach absorbed in our latest pocket-money scheme of collecting bottles from the beach to take back to the shop. This earned us sixpence per bottle so we thought this was good when added to using the camp-site as a venue for collecting things too. It was as we were walking on the beach though that it suddenly struck us that we could also have some fun by putting a message in a bottle and casting it out on the sea to goodness knows where!

Excited by this new found idea we hurried home and got out the paper and pens and began composing messages to throw in the water. After writing silly things, we settled down to just writing the plain facts about ourselves and giving our addresses to would finders to get in touch. These were carefully in numerous plastic bags then deposited in hardy plastic bottles with well fitting tops and dutifully taken to the beach.

We went to the furthest part of land from the sea and then, with all our might we flung them into the water, feeling rather pleased with ourselves that we had at last done something constructive with our day. I remember we stayed out there at that far cove searching for queenie shells, which we know we could use to decorate boxes and other simple items. After a while we made our way back across the beach to go home again. Imagine our HUGE disappointment when we discovered at our feet our own bottles, lying there begging to be discovered. We had thrown our bottles into an incoming tide and they had reached the shore before us! But that wasn't the end of the story – oh no!

When roger heard our story and saw how sad we were, he suggested that we write the messages again and prepare them for their journey. When he went out on his next trip from Falmouth down to the Suez Canal, he would throw them overboard along the way. He did carry out his promise, and threw three bottles off the boat when off the Spanish coast.

This was back in 1965.

In 1968 we received a letter from Sweden to say that they had found our messages thrown into the sea three years earlier! We were flabbergasted. Enclosed was this sweet picture of a young Swedish boy looking up at me, the original message and his address – to get in touch. We stayed in touch for a time but eventually lost contact as school exams and school work took over. However, my mum stayed in contact with is sister who came over to visit us all on one occasion.

We also had a reply from a finder of a bottle that ended up in the Manchester Shipping Canal, but this recipient was an older schoolmaster who didn't look so exciting, so it wasn't followed up.

September 16ᵗʰ 1963

If you find this
bottle please write
to this Address
R. 1. Luxton
M.V Chesterbrook
Comben longstaff Ltd
27 St Mary Axe
London E.C.3.

P.S. This was thrown
in to the sea of
Spain.

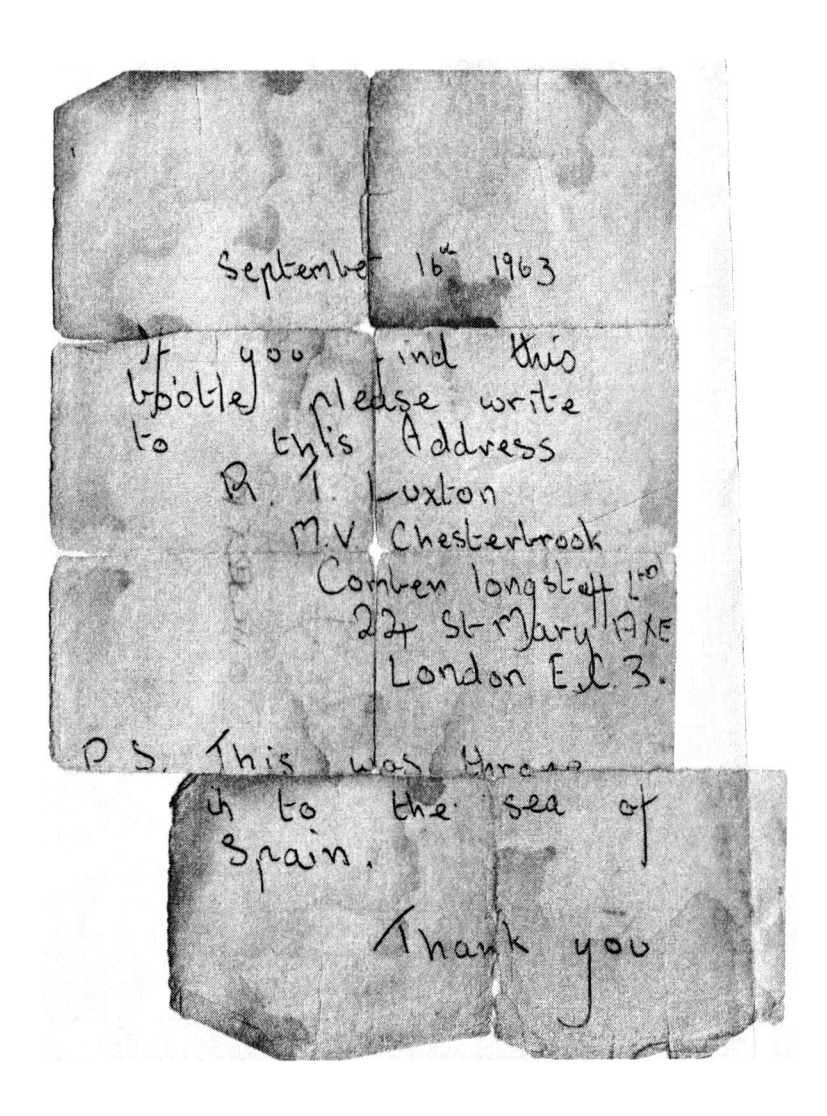

Thank you

Letter sent to sea in the bottle

> den 6/10-68
>
> Hello!
> I'm a Swedish boy 18
> years old. I fond your
> bottle in the water in
> a town called Lysekil
> on the Swedish westcoast.
>
> My adress
>
> L. A. Axelsson
> Box 23
> 45033 Grundsund
> Sweden

Response from Sweden

Family Barbecues

What joyous occasions these turned out to be; first we had to choose the right date that fitted in with the times of the tides, the one where the sea would cover the hot sand and then turn and go out in the early evening, guaranteeing that the water would be nice and warm for us all to have an evening dip.

The sandy field above the beach was always full of broccoli boxes, so dad and Lyn's father would throw a few over the edge to set up our bonfire. All the other kids would gather more wood from the shoreline to make the fire spectacular.

This cove was in a unique position as the sea only rarely came into it, and so the flotsam and jetsam which was washed up with the tide, we could easily collect and over a matter of weeks, build up a nice collection. The hauling of the food and equipment over the sand to this far end was the biggest problem, so each child was assigned a bag to carry and everyone did their part.

There's nothing quite like a beach at night-time when the smell of the sand is fresh and it is tempting you to bring the beach alive for a second time in the day. Later on, when the fire has been coaxed into life and the cove is packed with just family and friends, time is allowed for the fire to die down a bit from its first initial blaze and a grill is placed over the glowing flames to cook the food.

But not before mum and Aunty Muriel don their aprons and tie scarves round their heads to keep out the smoke. Cries then fill the air of 'Who wants sausage? Who wants bacon? With onions? Make your mind up boy!' The evening seems to go on forever with extra material that keeps the fire burning until the sun goes down, and the fire is the only illumination around mirroring red, greasy, happy faces whose next wish is to go for a swim knowing that a dip in the warm water at night is indeed an invigorating experience.

So good in fact that once you were in the water you never wanted to come out. But as the fire gradually consumed all its energy and our arms and legs became tired, reluctantly the evening drew to a close and we took our tired bodies home to bed.

The beach was indeed an extension of our village and what a playground we had here, always safe, always happy and not knowing what it meant to be bored. We occupied ourselves with boat building competitions, and then seeing whose boat was built the strongest by placing it into the sea, where the weakest would sink almost immediately. Or we would go to visit the caves to see what we could find; there was always something different to do everyday, the list was endless.

Yet inevitably these days of innocence came to an end all too quickly, for on one sunny day when we were on the beach, the water was tempting us to go in for a swim, but we were only allowed in if there was an adult present. Luckily one of our mums came down in the afternoons with some snacks.

On this particular day the water was exceptionally low; to be able to walk around the group of rocks to the next cove was a bad sign. Seeing it was so hot we were allowed to just go to the edge of the water to cool down.

Because there was no swimming allowed we skipped the waves to get wet. Suddenly and without warning I gave out the loudest scream possible while clutching my leg.

I remember the pain was so bad I felt faint. I looked down to my foot which was now turning blue. mum came running up to me; she took one look and knew it was something serious. She told John to run to the farm as quickly as possible to get someone down to the beach.

It seemed to take forever before I heard adults' voices coming towards us. By now I was lying down suffering an even worse pain than before. mum lifted my leg to examine my foot more closely, which had become even more blue in colour. Soon the reason for all the drama was discovered, for there on my skin were two puncture marks made by a weaver fish and its poisonous spines. I must have accidentally stepped on it, making it pierce my skin with its spines releasing poison into my foot and up my leg.

Before I knew what was happening there was a bowl of steaming hot water beside me and mum was encouraging me to put my foot in it; it was the only cure and soon my foot and leg had returned to their natural colour and the purple poison subsided.

Even to this day, I never go near the water when the tide is exceptionally low, as more than likely there are little weaver fish buried in the sand with just their spines showing, ready to inject the unsuspecting swimmer with their poison.

On dull days we were to be found catching little fish and shrimps in the rock pools and digging our fingers into the sea anemones, so that we might watch as they shrank from sight, then fearfully emerge again so that we might repeat this cruel trick; what horrible children we were sometimes.

The beach filled our days completely and left us with many happy recollections, yet with the balance of life, as it gave to us, on one fateful occasion so it took its share.

The day dawned much the same as any other; it wasn't fiercely hot but nice enough to waste a few hours looking for anything the sea might have washed up. So we were lazily exploring when we first noticed a bit of a commotion taking place on the opposite side of the beach.

There was a lot of hand waving going on and we could hear shouting too, so inquisitively we made our way over to that side to see what was going on and soon wished we had stayed put where we were.

On the rocks there was a girl crying hysterically and pointing to the water. We didn't know these kids very well; they lived on the opposite side of the village to us and were never around much because they went away to boarding school and returned home for the holidays.

Her brother had gone to get help because their sister had fallen into the water. We looked down to the rocks below but couldn't see anything. The water was crashing on the rocks and we were a long way from the shore.

The next thing we heard was a roaring in the sky and there was a helicopter above us, creating a massive gale with its rotors that nearly blew us away, so we made our way back to the shore and just watched from there.

They circled around and around the spot for ages, then the man we had seen inside the helicopter was being lowered close down to the water on a rope and what we witnessed next will stick in my mind for all of my life.

The rope and the man were being winched back into the helicopter and he was holding something in his arms, but all we could see was dangling long blonde hair and drooping legs. The helicopter stayed very low then came in our direction onto the beach.

With the sand being flung out in all directions it landed on the beach. The noise was tremendous, but before we had time to catch our breath it was taking off again. We never did know why it stopped on the beach. The next thing we were conscious of was our mothers running towards us.

They must have heard all the action and hoped the victim of the sea was not one of their own children. Later we established that it was a local girl who drowned; apparently she had lost her hair band and had gone into the water to retrieve it, not wanting to return home without it. Sadly this action cost her life.

This was something we all took a long time to get over, but then we had more respect for our delightful beach understanding that there really was a thin line between life and death.

Soon we left our childhood behind and became young adults in a world of responsibility and seriousness we were not to forget.

Lasse Axel Axellson, the Swedish boy who answered the message with his baby sister

Chapter Three
THE SCHOOL YEARS

Infant School

We all went to the same Infant School though. This was in Goldsithney, the next village on from ours. If it was dry weather we would all walk the mile together, all gathering at Little Plantation which was a clump of trees on the outskirts of the village before the slog up Perran Hill.

In the winter though, when the weather was rough, we were able to have a lift in Mr Laity's car. This was a Morris Oxford and it seemed huge inside to us as we all piled in. He would drop us outside the school on the path that led up to the entrance.

In the early days of attending school I would cry my eyes out every morning, which was a peculiar thing to do, since I really enjoyed myself once I got there.

The reason I was so upset everyday was because I was leaving my mother behind at home and I thought she might be lonely there all day on her own. After assurances from her that she had plenty to do during the day and the time just flew by for her I was more settled.

Class of 1959

My classmates were a motley crew: Lyn and Shiela Bettens were farmers' daughters; I was the farmworker's daughter; John Sewell's dad was a mechanic; the Hosking boys – Anthony, Philip and Kevin – were the landowner's sons, and we had gypsy children from the local site, whom we were told not to speak to.

I sat next to a girl called Carol Thomas. She was tall and skinny and I disliked her for some reason. At break-times I was always glad to be back with Lyn. But sometimes Lyn was friendly with a girl called Sabrina Badcock, so those times I had to play with someone else.

I was friendly with one of the boys, Stephen Basher. His parents, Jack and Vera, owned the garage in the village. We all empathised with Stephen, because he couldn't move quite as freely as the rest of us, having callipers on his legs, and often went home for tea at Paul and John's house. He was a whiz at playing French Cricket though, because all he had to do was to swipe the ball with his metal frame and not bother with a bat up close like the rest of us, so he could be half way to scoring points before the rest of us even knew where the ball had gone.

He was always fun to be with and never moaned about his predicament when we were all crowded round him. Sadly though Stephen never lived longer than these early school days and as I used his parents' garage for petrol when I had a car of my own, his mum would inevitably serve me and always commented that Stephen would have been my age now, and say perhaps how he might have grown up and have done different things with his life. I was always sad too when I thought of him and wondered how he would have been at my age; that's the thing about life, we have to say goodbye to the people we like or love sad as it is, that's the way it goes.

We filled our break-times with a variety of activities: hoola hoops, sticky toffee, tag, hopscotch and Jacks. But by the time we were queueing up for our chocolate fingers, digestives and milk, break-time seemed to have gone and soon we were being ushered back in for lessons again.

On wet cold winter days we were allowed to stay in over break-time and raid the comic box or fish out the nicest toys to play with. Also we could have hot milk. Miss Mayes would take each third-of-a-pint bottle and rest them up around the edge of the huge boiler that dominated the room keeping us warm, so that was a nice treat.

Our classroom of twenty-five to thirty was one big room enclosing us all; it seemed like a big cave. Although the sign over the entrance said boys one way and girls the other we were always together, sitting facing the teacher with all of us being divided in rows of desks with two at each one.

I remember Miss Mayes as being lovely and she always smelt like the aroma of Camay soap.

We recited a lot of tables here and we had spellings to take home to learn. I remember being the proud owner of my first reading book; it was all about the *Adventures of Janet and John.* Even at this early age I was conscious of rushing through my reading and writing so that I might spend a few precious minutes in the reading corner before lunch, reading my favourite books on my own.

Then in the afternoons we would have a time of playing with our toys and have a little sleep if we were tired.

At the end of the day we would have a special story read to us – stories about *Rikki Tikki Tavi*, the mongoose, and also the adventures of the *Famous Five*.

When I started reading at home, my favourite ones were always about animals. There was one special one, *Black Beauty*, which I read over and over again, but it had to be prised away from me because it made me cry so much. Following on from the *Famous Five* I devoured all the *Secret Seven* books and would make up unbelievable stories of our gang's adventures, only to be told that I really did have a vivid imagination.

There was also another lady who helped Miss Mayes in the classroom, Mrs Green, who was always there in the mornings to greet us and help us with our coats and outdoor shoes, I remember her as being more matronly than our teacher who would hover on the sidelines of the classroom ready to come to anyone's assistance. This was usually Miriam Whitford who could never keep up with the rest of us.

The thought of her reminded me of a horrible thing she did one day while we were having lunch; she suddenly sent out this enormous sneeze that flew across the table covering everything, including the pasty she was eating. Ugh! It was horrendous; it made us all feel sick and put us off pasties for a very long time. I still see her sometimes and whenever I do, I always remember that dinner time at my school in '59.

A person I did single out as a new friend was a girl called Phillipa Curnow. Her mother was the local post woman. I always looked forward to going to her house for tea, but we always had the same thing – baked beans on toast – which I thought was a bit strange, so I asked her if she ever had anything different than beans for tea. She didn't like my remark so became really cross with me, so that was it, the invitations ceased to come. Phillipa had a sister called Caroline and one day it leaked out that they both had the middle name of Cavendish which in fact was a family name. We all thought this was a little strange so we nicknamed the two sister's 'Dishy'; it didn't go down very well and we got told off for it, followed by an apology.

Junior School

Yet all too soon we reached the fine old age of seven and had to move on to Junior School. It was rumoured that there was a fine school on the promenade in Penzance, St Mary's C of E, but as a lot of us were Methodists, our parents had to first seek permission for us to attend this school from the bishop of Truro.

Once this was done we had to arrange transport to get us from Perranuthnoe to Penzance Station, then onto a bus to get us over to the Promenade, but seeing as we were so young to start off with we had different parents taking it in turn to accompany us to school.

What adventures we had just travelling to school. We left Perran just after eight o'clock in the morning, and of course sometimes we missed it. We would run up to 'little crossroads' where two roads crossed over just before the bus stop by the pub, just to see the bus tail lights disappearing up Perran Hill. This didn't guarantee us missing school though; we would dash home and the car would be started and then there was a race to catch the bus up as it stopped at its numerous pick-up points on the way to Penzance.

But most of the time we would be the first ones to be picked up, so we would make a dash for the back seat. We could then look out the window and make faces at the innocent driver who happened to be following us.

At the Railway Station we all got off and had to surge forward as one, onto the Mousehole blue buses that travelled the scenic route along the prom to their destination. From the prom we had to walk the last bit of the way to school just as the bell was ringing.

Now St Mary's was a mansion compared to the tiny village school we had just left. Each year had their own classroom with its own teacher; there was an assembly hall which doubled up as the gym – or at least a space for P.E; and there was separate canteen on the front which fogged up in dull weather, being airless and windowless (and always smelling of boiled cabbage).

St Mary's had a lot to answer for in the amount of days off we had in our early school years.

To begin with, the toilets were situated at the furthest end of the playground which meant quite a battle, for the little children who were only seven, to fight their way across here with a force ten gale blowing that was trying to sweep them off in the opposite direction.

In fact once the door of the main building closed behind you on this great journey into the unknown there was never any hard-fast guarantee you might survive the ordeal back again.

Again if the weather was really bad and stormy in the 1960s, in the days before the walls of the promenade were reinforced against the seas offences, the raging storm water tore over the promenade, washed over the road, through the row of houses and ended up in the school canteen.

On slightly better days in the winter, the frosts would take over and again it was the toilets that were most badly affected as they would freeze over and again school would be cancelled.

On one occasion during such stormy weather, we battled to school thinking the day would be rough but not impossible... to be told that yes... it was business as usual, only to witness the day deteriorate weather wise, turning into hurricane storm conditions; teachers paled as they struggled to be heard against screeching winds and lashing rain, but when tiles started crashing off roofs then it was decided to call it a day.

Parents were called to come to fetch their children only to find that roads had been flooded and diversions had been put in place. Two cars were assigned to fetch the Perran and Goldsithney children; we were instructed to stay indoors until our lift came, then when we eventually went out the whole landscape was transformed in front of our very eyes.

Waves that had been born and formed miles out in the Atlantic were still bashing cruelly down into our playground. The very road we had walked along just a matter of hours ago was now flooded with several feet of water and there in the middle of it all was our headmistress, covered from head to foot in oilers and sloshing about in yellow wellingtons trying to direct children into the waiting cars.

The force of the wind was trying to knock us over, like we were mere pawns in a chess game, and the rain beat down ferociously, taking our breath away; even if you did keep your mouth closed as instructed it shot in your eyes and up your nostrils.

I remember the noise of the storm rising above everything else, stamping out the sound of the teachers' voices as they tried to give out their instructions. Then the cars started to arrive, looking like boats floating through the rainwater. We had to manoeuvre the pavement and the gurgling storm drains to get to the door of the car, and then produce a lot of strength to pull open the car door. But eventually we all piled inside, our wet clothes squeaking against the leather seats as we sat down, but so relieved and lucky to be going home.

There were various teachers whose names come to mind as I recall these days. The headmistress, Miss Girling, was a tyrant; we had to do italic writing, which took a lot of time and effort. We had to use these special pens where the nib was on a slant; they produced lovely work, but took a long time to do. Yet our writing went 'to pot' at college as we ferociously hurried to take notes. So all this time doing italic writing was wasted.

Then it dawned on me that the writing had to look nice just for show and other activities we did went towards this common aim.

We engaged in long assemblies at this C of E School; they were usually taken by the vicar, Father Sargisson, and older members of the school read various lessons, attended by the school choir.

Then after this we had a morning of Scripture so that eventually I knew the Bible inside out, which was probably a good thing in our religious family.

But with the knowledge came questioning, which was rather embarrassing in the family, yet Grandpa Joe could always support a good discussion, although, I think it left some doubt in the omnipotent belief we all had to have in God.

Another teacher who shaped these younger school days of mine was called Miss Savage. Unfortunately for me I discovered that her temperament was just as savage as her name. I enjoyed her music class; I mastered playing the recorder that most Junior children did, but when it came to writing down the musical score the real fun began... or not, as the case may be.

My greatest challenge at this time was in mastering the curves and lines of the treble cleft. The more times I attempted it the worse I got; I started with its tail, then up, around and curl around to finish... but it always went the wrong way and the more I rubbed it out the thinner the paper became until horror of horrors... I rubbed right through the paper then I cried my big wet snotty tears.

Miss Savage got into just as much of a state as me; she said the state of the page was disgusting, then she tore the page out, screwed it up into a ball and threw it into a bin, throwing the remains of the rest of the book right in my face.

I was reduced to a quivering wreck and was left in the classroom on my own all playtime, practising page after page of treble clefts. The humiliation and indignation I felt were awful. She never liked me from that moment and the feeling was certainly mutual. I left the choir and never played the recorder again, or any sort of musical instrument, until my secondary school.

Then there was Miss Uren. She took the little ones and had all the patience in the world, peering over thick-rimmed glasses at you. Her lovely soft pink skin matched her soft personality. I would have liked to have stayed in her class all my way through Junior School, but of course had to move through the grades as I got older. That didn't stop me volunteering to help out in her classroom though, when the occasion arose or if the little ones needed extra tuition.

Overall I can honestly say that these school days were happy ones and generally it was the good times that outnumbered the bad; there was not one thing that I would make up excuses for to not go in the next day, although I was always glad when the school holidays arrived, especially on one occasion when I was chosen to take the class pets home to look after while the school was shut.

Not that you can really call stick insects pets; a pet to me was like my beloved cat, Pandy, whom you could stroke, cuddle, groom and love.

In the classroom these insects were kept in a large plastic sweet container with holes punched in the lid. They were kept on the windowsill in the shade and sometimes when I became a bit bored with my work, I would look up to look at them; they would be gathered together on their branches and looked just like twigs that were imprisoned in their forest, watching us creatures glued to our desks imprisoned in our work.

Sometimes the teacher would coax them out to pose for us and get them to run up her arms bringing them to life.

As the end of term grew nearer the teacher was tentatively asking who might be free to take the pets home for the summer holidays. When I discovered that all you needed to do to care for them was to clean them out daily and provide fresh privet for them to eat, I thought I might like to give it a go.

After all we had lots of privet growing on the hedges on the lane down to Boat cove, so when I was given permission from mum to look after them, I swore to the teacher on my life they would be O.K.

So on the last day of term I balanced all the old work that had accumulated over the weeks to go home, plus a dinosaur model we had been studying and grasped the sweet jar and set off for the bus.

When I got home, as usual my cat Pandy was waiting for me, and walked the short distance to my door. Once inside the cottage the entire lot of work was emptied onto the kitchen table.

The sweet jar took pride of place in the middle of the rubbish. Pandy expressed great interest in the jar by sniffing all around it and, when he saw something actually move inside, he decided to post himself on watch so that nothing could get in or out of his domain.

When it was time for me to clean them out it was a major campaign; the jar was unceremoniously tipped upside down to shake the creatures out who were plainly terrified at their abrupt treatment and clung on to their old habitat for dear life.

After getting rid of all the old mess the new privet was pushed in and the creatures were given a bit of a run on the lino. Pandy, my dearest friend during these holidays, would sit on the perimeter of the room, not daring to move; he would just watch fascinated as these lumbering creatures would sway across the floor looking for shelter.

Occasionally I would come back from some journey out and find the cat sitting beside the jar mesmerised, as its contents pretended to be sticks and then inevitably getting bored and changing their positions by just stretching their legs. Pandy would paw the plastic wanting some playmate to keep him amused but eventually gave up on them, as there was no action there.

Anyway, one Sunday morning after a bit of a lie in, sheer horror greeted my dad's eyes as he entered the kitchen; it was a scene of unrivalled chaos. Privet leaves and branches were strewn around the room, bits of plastic were all over the place, and in the middle of the mess in a little pile, was a mound of stick insects' legs.

Panda had torn their home to pieces and eaten the bodies and had the audacity to leave their remains there as a prize for me to show that he had conquered the in-house tenants once and for all.

The conqueror had the sense to leave the scene of the crime and now was nowhere around; but his trail of destruction led to the open window. So there was no doubt that he was the instigator of the whole thing!

I was so upset when I realised the full extent of the tragedy and understood that the whole thing must have been my fault, as I couldn't have put the lid on securely when I changed their food.

Pandy must have prised the lid off and got a secure grip on the jar, and then taken it apart with his teeth. Poor little stick insects!

My mother took me to school on the first day of the new term; she led me into my new class and in her abrupt voice urged me to confess the Stick Insect incident to Miss Savage, who took an instant dislike to me from that day and I never had the opportunity to take anything living home with me again.

New term brought a new friend for me. I met a girl here whom I became very friendly with over the remaining years. Her name was Althea Mckenzie and she lived at Newlyn in Penzance. her dad was an artist and they had a nice house which looked out over Newlyn harbour. I especially liked to go home and have tea with her because from out of the window I could glance out over the harbour below, and imagine that my brother Roger was sailing into port as we played.

At this time I was very close to my older brother; there was an age gap between us of about ten years, but he had finished school as soon as he could and gone to sea. My mother begged him not to leave us so soon, so he did work on the land until the age of seventeen, and then went to Technical College on a part-time course to learn engineering.

After that there was no holding him back; first of all he was out from Newlyn on the 'Brook' boats. The reason they were called this was because all their names ended in 'Brook', his first boat being the *Chesterbrook*, owned by the company Cobham & Longstaff of London.

He would take stone abroad to the continent from Newlyn quarry and he would always bring me back a miniature doll dressed in its country's traditional dress. I still have them displayed at home.

But of course I used to worry about him just like my mum did; I don't know why, because when we were young I used to start fights with him and he used to always get the blame.

Even so on those rough winter days in school assembly when we were singing, 'For those in peril on the sea', my thoughts would picture him bobbing up and down on a rough sea, all alone somewhere and I would end up with tears streaming down my face for no reason.

He would say, 'You mustn't worry about me. If its rough where you are, we are probably somewhere calm or berthed up somewhere and vice versa: if it's good weather at home, we might be riding out a storm, but you wouldn't even be thinking about us then, so no worries.'

I'm afraid that my status as being the 'mistake' in the family hierarchy was turning around so that now I was being labelled the spoilt one and could do no harm, whilst my brother was establishing himself as the independent one and my sister was the one stuck in the middle.

When I was eleven I lost my innocence in so many ways; it was the time that I was coming up to leaving my Junior School and it was a struggle to decide where to go for my Secondary Education.

Here fate once again took a hand in deciding where I should move. In the days of taking the eleven plus all my friends and I at St Mary's had to take this exam, but unfortunately the results of this weren't black and white for me.

It was rumoured that I was a 'borderline' case, then other factors came into play. At the interview, first of all I was summoned into the Headmistress's office. Shaking with fright I knocked on the door to be greeted by stern, gruff voices.

I was told to sit on one of the hard wooden chairs in front of all the staff, then I was asked all sorts of questions about my life, my family and my hobbies. I left the office very sad and sure that I had done something wrong.

In the end it was thought that I had failed this testing because when it came to the crunch, I didn't really belong to the 'right' class.

I wondered endlessly what this meant and learnt that on the whole only the 'better' educated went to Grammar School.

Up until now when my friends and I were playing in our small village we were all the same; we all lived in stable families, all went to chapel and Sunday School and acted alike.

I didn't have the slightest idea what class was or meant; it seemed like a dirty word or one not to be mentioned in the house. Even when my friend, Lyn, went off to a West Cornwall school – St Erbyns, and wore a brown uniform with a straw hat in the summer which she wasn't allowed to take off, I still didn't catch onto the idea that we were different from each other.

I was even too stupid coming up to eleven to realise that there was a real difference between the farmer's daughter and the Farm worker's daughter and we would be seen as quite different from each other in the future, although we still played together quite contentedly at the weekends and in the holidays.

So it was that I went to Heamoor Secondary School, still with some of my friends from Junior School: namely Carol Thomas, Philippa Curnow and Althea McKenzie and meekly accepted my state.

I was quite happy with these friends and I met more new friends and of course it was the introduction of boys to my life too; we all had our crushes of course. Mainly it was a culture shock, coming from our four friendly classrooms to a building where we mixed with 500 other people, where we experienced a life of lessons in technical drawing, drama, physics, science, woodwork and domestic science.

There were three floors of rooms and winding corridors where we continually got lost; really we were the small fish in this big pond, but quickly found our feet and settled in.

Also the other milestone at eleven was when I won the *Daily Mirror* literary competition for a story I only got a certificate for. I don't even remember what the subject was but straight away I had an affinity with English.

It was my best subject and the two English teachers, Miss Easton and Mr Burton, who I had during this time, encouraged me enormously, saying that I had a wide imagination and would 'go far' in the subject. I also liked the boys but didn't suffer them lightly.

One, who would cycle over to Perran to visit, would want me to meet him in secret, so once I climbed out the bedroom window and went down to the beach to meet him; although I got home in good time, I lied to my mother about where I had been. Once she found out I was lying she put a total ban on our meetings, which only made me sneak into town on a Saturday to go to the pictures with him.

Another one used to follow our school bus down Market Jew Street in the evenings on his bike and we would all huddle in the back seat making faces at him and blowing him kisses! It was all just a bit of fun and didn't come to anything.

Then there were the dances at the Grammar School. Now that was something else; there was a balcony high up around the dance floor and a shiny silver ball that reflected patterns all around the room; we had competitions to see who could snog the most boys during the course of the evening and boast about our achievements on the Monday mornings.

We all started our periods around the same time and thought we were all really grown up and quite superior to the boys anyway, followed by the uphill struggle with exams and what our next step would be in the academic world.

We were told that C.S.E. Exams (Certificate in Secondary Education) grade one was definitely the equivalent to an 'O' level and with me it was the struggle again to show that I was equal to the Grammar School people.

Nobody was more surprised when I opened my envelope on the day of the results to find that I had five grade ones, the best in school, whereas some of my friends at Grammar had only scraped in with their results.

It was only later that reality struck me that when asked how many exams we've achieved, all we did was to just record the subjects, no one asked which grades we had got anyway.

I decided to go to Technical College at Camborne and try for some 'A' Levels in my best subjects of English, History and R.E. Also this was a time when I was coming up to driving age so my brother helped by buying a car for me, and what a beauty it was!

I had a Morris Minor; it was an old one with a split windscreen and a tiny window at the back. My dad went out with me in the evenings and basically taught me to drive but wasn't exactly blessed with loads of patience and I had to finish off with some professional lessons to pass my test.

It still took me three times to pass it though and the first time I was let loose on my own, I scraped the car coming around a narrow road and nearly gave up completely. Yet after this minor hiccup, I did gain the confidence to drive a few of my mates to college.

The poor old car was showing its age by now; when it rained we had to have umbrellas up turned upside down in the front to catch the water leaking through the windscreen, so this was traded in before long for a Mini.

Again, I moulded into this model and only gave it up a few years later out of necessity, when I was too pregnant to squeeze behind the wheel.

From my three years at Tech, I gained three 'A' levels and was on my way towards my ambition of becoming a teacher.

My friend Lyn was also following a similar career; she was accepted at Bath Domestic Science College and I got into Worcester Teachers Training College. The trouble was it was so far from home, being six hours on the train and near to Birmingham. It opened yet another chapter in my life.

Chapter Four
GRANDPA JOE/A LIFE ON THE TWIST

What can you say about Grandpa Joe?

Here he was this little man of eight stone with the strength of a lion and a character that held a personality that would always be remembered as a strong figurehead of our village.

He had many passions, one of which was turning the soil of the field with his trusty astronomic, gentle and graceful pair of shire horses. Beautifully harnessed together, hour after hour they trudged up and down each furrow taking Grandpa Joe with them. He never looked heavy enough to control these, being no higher than a hob, and beside this pair of beautiful horses he looked the size of an ant as the pair towered above him.

He seemed at his happiest when he was cultivating the land, and with the sea view visible just over the cliff it must have been the most relaxing experience in its way.

From turning the soil in the field, he would work long hours in another field where he planted, tended and nurtured all kinds of vegetables for the family and most of the residents of the village.

He also was a mainstay in the violet trade; preparing the ground, seeking out the healthiest plants for planting, endlessly he would work until his old bones became too tired to bend over, so he would spread out his old sack that he kept tied around his waist and kneel on the soil between each row ready to pick blooms.

All members of the family worked on the land whatever their age. When us women on the rare occasion thought it was too wet, cold and windy to spend time working in the field, Grandpa Joe would always be there with a scarf tied round his hat to keep it on and singing hymns to himself. He could recount all the hymns in the Methodist book and had a fine voice. He had held the post of steward of the local chapel so was always there for the two Sunday services; one at 2.15 the other at 5.45. He felt honoured in such a position to be able to be there to open the doors and make the place welcoming for the visiting preachers.

Grandpa Joe taking a break on the farm

But as age got a hold on him, his hearing became impaired and poor Grandpa Joe would end up being one verse behind the rest of the congregation. As we finished the song with an Amen, he would still be happily going on until he noticed our cue to sit down.

Sundays were always sacrosanct in the days of my childhood; there was no nipping down to the beach after the service for a quick swim in our best clothes. Temptation was made worse by the fact that the chapel was right on the beach road, just a few hundred yards from it. We found it hard to even concentrate on the service in hand, with the sound of the trippers passing by outside.

Usually the preacher would come over to our house afterwards and take tea with us, so we had no choice but to be on our best behaviour for the whole day. It remained an unwritten law that all members of every family always went to chapel for the two services; the only time you were excused from this was when you were confined to your bed with some illness.

My brother Roger at this time was working for small fishing boats out of Newlyn; he was a qualified engineer and would go out on trips limited to about a week out then a few days in and so on.

Of course a lot depended on the weather; during the winter gales few boats left the confinement of the harbour, but made up for this when the weather improved.

My brother I think, was born with the sea water in his veins; he either had to be on the sea fishing or fishing from the rocks at Boat Cove to be happy.

He would have never been an academic studying in the confines of a classroom; he was always at his happiest when he was outdoors. After crewing on these small vessels he progressed to bigger boats – taking stone from the Newlyn Quarry around to Wales.

He always hated this Sunday ritual, and would think up any excuse possible to get out of going. I remember on one particular afternoon his friends had all agreed to meet up to go fishing. Well in the build up of getting washed and changed for the afternoon service, he 'accidentally' dropped the bowl of hot soapy water he was carrying up to his bedroom, spilling the contents from the top to the bottom, causing a 'mini' flood in the well at the bottom of the stairs.

After being scolded for his actions, he was told to stay at home to clean up the mess he had made. For this he was silently grateful, yet, when we all returned home later he was nowhere to be seen; the mess had been cleared up immaculately, but it was some time before he returned carrying a basket full to the brim with fresh mackerel, which he used to appease my mother into forgiving him for not attending the day's service. But the best part of the day was when we all tucked into a good feast that night.

Grandpa Joe was under the impression that Roger had missed the services because of a cold, but was soon informed that actually he had returned to Newlyn to catch the next tide out taking him out to sea for a week, where upon his return his recent incident would have been forgotten.

Eventually Roger got his own boat and started taking tourists for trips around Mount's Bay where they could catch their own fish. If there was any surplus left, he would take them around the village and up to the campsite where he would sell them for twenty to fifty pence each, depending whether he liked the tripper or not.

Whenever he landed a good catch we would all meet him down at Boat Cove and gather together any bits of wood to make a fire. The fish feast straight from the sea was slowly cooked and enjoyed by all, which included Grandpa Joe, who would sit overseeing the proceedings from the old men's wooden bench that was perched by the boat shed, a favourite place shared by the old men of the village: Percy, Jan Brewer Pebble eye and Willy Bray. They would come and all gather there on summer evenings, telling their tales of wrecks, ghosts and unnatural happenings, always shocking the passing tourists.

Percy Curnow could transform a tripper to a gibbering wreck if he was in the mood to shock all with his most convincing tale of the day. One such tale was when he entered the church one bright summer's day to be confronted by a very cold interior and on journeying into the vestry to put the heaters on, found a ghost blocking his way.

When asked to move by Percy, the ghost said that this was as much his house as those who came here, so Percy continued with his duties of placing the hymn books in the pews and checking that the prayer mats were in order, with, he claims, the ghost's cold eyes following his every action.

When he came to shifting a certain mat belonging to a former churchwarden, he felt a icy presence surrounding him and the prayer mat moved from where he had put it.

Percy would then take great pains to tell the entranced audience exactly which seat was affected by this occurrence and dared them with his eyes to visit the church on their return journey from the cove and sit in this same seat.

Most trippers swallowed this story – hook, line and sinker, not knowing the real fact, perhaps, that Percy was inclined to enjoy a decent downing of Guinness in the local on most Saturday nights and spun stories such as these to vulnerable visitors after such sprees.

Pebble Eye was another good old Cornish fisherman of the old kind, and he was never to be outdone when such stories were being related. Now this man had this nickname because he had such terrible eyesight with the result that the glasses he wore had the thickness of jam jars.

We believe he actually saw very little of the real world, but insisted on driving a tiny three wheeler between Boat Cove and his home along the main road a couple of miles away.

He was a big man and would squeeze himself into his little car for these vital journeys, but to ask him how his sight became so bad was to embark on a tale that could last up to an hour in the telling – according on his mood, and how captive his audience were.

His story began when he was a small boy; his father had taken him fishing right on this very spot, when suddenly, there, yes, just in front of where we are now, he would say, up through that fishing channel there, glided up this great monster of the deep. 'Aye it must have been nigh on a quarter of a mile long, you could count the humps along his back boy!' he would say accentuating the tale by flaying his arms in all directions.

Then... his father's line would tighten and he'd declare he'd caught this monster – the devil's spawn – on the end. Pebble Eye was then instructed to wade into the channel and see if he might loosen the hook from the monster's jaws saying, 'Quick boy, afore he do turn tail and take us all with him into the deep!' So Pebble Eye followed his father's instructions and enters the water to confront the 'monster', which is in fact a Conger eel. Yet as he grapples with the fish, the latter splashes up in his face and hits him full in the eyes where a hook becomes embedded.

It is up to his father to wriggle the hook out and help his injured son to safety – but in this process the eel frees itself from their grip, turns tail and quickly disappears into deeper water.

It was feared that Pebble Eye might have lost his sight completely but is fortunate that he is left able to see hazy outlines – made better, of course, by wearing his faithful glasses for life.

So his story will conclude eventually – depending on the actual size of the eel on the day – and the swiftness of his father's reactions, 'The Lord above chose to spare me and to protect his waters here for all to enjoy, praise his name.'

On the ending of this fishy tale the tourists would look towards the seas with mouths aghast, wondering if clumps of seaweed locked in motion with the ebb and flow of the tide might be monsters under the water caught in the current forever.

Brother Jack will then follow their gaze and ask apprehensively who is up for the next journey out of the bay; only the most hardy trippers will find sufficient courage to follow him down to the boat to board – wondering if they might trust this old codger to bring them back safely if they consent to going with him.

The old wooden bench was like a memorial to the old men, especially Grandpa Joe and his good friend Percy. They would sit there for hours comparing vegetable prices at the local market and argue the latest treatment of crop disease. To them black was white when it came to religion. Percy was the curator of the C of E Church whereas Grandpa, being the warden of the Methodist Chapel, could never agree when defining the two.

We might have all lived in a sleepy little village which on the surface gave the appearance that nothing much happened there, but Grandpa Joe was certainly the most knowledgeable individual there was. He could tell you the state of the tide or the moon in an instant; not only which direction the wind was coming from, but if it was likely to change and what the weather would be like in the next couple of days. He was a power to revere.

Grandpa Joe & Grandpa Issac

Getting some Bite into the Ginger Beer Plants

Grandpa Joe's enjoyable habit was a good old smoke and it was rumoured that he got into it before he even reached his teens, but his faithful old pipe was always to be found in his pocket for easy access. He smoked a mixture called 'Twist' which got its name from being sold in a long thin strip like liquorice, which was required to be cut to size to the smoker's requirements.

The ritual that preceded the smoke was one that had to be seen to be believed. The first step was to clean the bowl of his pipe, using his red-spotted handkerchief – a cloth for many things, which included ear cleaning, blowing his nose and wiping sweat from his forehead.

This done he would take out his multi-purpose penknife, wipe the blade on his scruffy, corduroy breeches and then proceed to cut up the 'Twist' into manageable pieces. He would then press this down into his pipe and light up, which took many matches before the tobacco would smoke, causing the immediate vicinity to be enveloped in a sweet smelling sea of tobacco fumes that clouded all sense of being. Some would say it looked like 'tobacco smog'.

The effect on the passive non-smokers in the immediate environment was that of sighs, grunts and coughing as the outline of familiar sights became blurred in the fusing between reality and smoke, as they were forced to become passive participants in his 'Twist moment'. For all of his smoking he was a picture of health and never had a day's illness in his life, living well into his nineties.

He lived with my Aunty Muriel and Uncle Bill just up the road from us, but every evening he would wander the short distance down the hill, carrying his slippers in his hands to join us to watch the nine o'clock news.

Grandpa Joe and the Rat

On one particular evening he had forgotten to bring down their enamel milk can that my dad would take down to the farm first thing in the morning when he went to work.

We were all preoccupied with the news when suddenly the door burst open and there stood my aunty with the can in her hand. 'You forgot this,' she said holding up the can. Then suddenly she stopped short in her tracks, her face turning really pale.

'Come in,' we all told her, but Aunty Muriel was frozen on the spot; she stood there pointing her finger towards the piano in the corner of the room.

'What's up maid, you look like you've seen a ghost?' Grandpa Joe asked her, but Muriel was speechless while still pointing at the piano.

'In there, a rat just went in behind the piano,' she directed.

'Don't be silly, you're imagining it, come and sit down and I'll make you a nice cup of tea.'

My mother tutted and led aunty to the chair and placed her tea down on it, but she still kept her eyes fixed on that piano. We all thought she was having a funny turn until at last my dad called to my brother to come and help him shift the piano, 'cause summit had crawled behind it.

Roger reluctantly joined dad and together they heaved the great iron-framed piano over to the side so they could see behind. Nothing was found. They even took a look inside.

'There, satisfied? It was your imagination after all,' suggested the men, and Aunty Murial was sent home for the night.

The next day mum was preparing to go shopping on the bus. She took out her shopping bag and set it down while she wrote out her shopping list. As she was writing something caught her eye. Was her brain playing tricks with her or did her shopping bag just move? She didn't wait to find out and fled the room in haste.

Nearby she spied some roofers repairing a neighbour's roof. They were a couple of young lads. She strode right up to them and shouted, 'Excuse me! Eh, can you help? I think there might be a rat in my shopping bag and I'm afraid to look!'

The boys eyed one another, made a few faces and started to descend from the roof.

'Of course missus, just show us where he is.'

They stealthily carried the bag from the kitchen to the garden and timidly turned it upside down.

'Nothing! It's empty... better take more water with it next time,' they declared, and they stifled a laugh as they made their way back.

Red-faced mum took the bag and list and did her shopping. That evening Aunty Muriel came down to visit again looking all about her as she entered the sitting room. 'Oh my God,' she squealed.

It was very unusual to hear Aunty say such words, especially when Grandpa Joe was present, but there as clear as day and visible for all to see was the rat. He ran out from the room making for the kitchen.

Silently we all followed, not quite sure what we were going to do. We watched the tail disappear behind the new fridge, mum's pride and joy. She quickly shut the kitchen door, sure that we had cornered the enemy.

Her next reaction was to scoop up the peacefully asleep cat and shove him in the kitchen too. Poor Pandy cried and yelped, followed by much screeching, then made for the open window and was gone.

The next person summoned was Uncle Bill. All the men armed themselves with cricket stumps and marched into the kitchen. The first thing they did was to move the fridge and as they did, so the rat shot free and latched on to the first thing he came in contact with, which was Grandpa Joe's slipper.

Grandpa danced around the kitchen, simultaneously vigorously shaking his foot. But the rat wouldn't budge. He did manage eventually to get the slipper off, and all set in to daze the creature. Grandpa was as dazed as the rat and most upset over the destruction of his newly bought slipper, but there was relief all around at least for a while anyway. But worse was to follow when mum and dad went to bed that night.

It was a bit chilly so mum had cause to approach the spare bed that was placed in the corner of their room. Well shock and horror, as mum went to pull our a spare blanket from the ready-made bed, she found that the rat had made its nest there, right under their noses, and they had been sleeping in the same room, night after night unaware of its presence.

All had to eat humble pie and say sorry to Aunty Muriel, admitting that she was right after all. The new fridge, like Grandpa's slipper, was ruined and a stark lesson was learned by all: always investigate imagined stories of any creatures that might be sharing your home with you.

Grandpa Joe came down the following night on the dot at nine, like he always did, but this time he had no slippers in his hand; he was going to have to get a new pair. The rat situation was not mentioned. All he said was his usual greeting of 'Evening all', just like the actor that was in a popular police drama at the time called, *Dixon of Dock Green*. His chair would always be waiting for him beside the fire so that he could take up a warm and comfortable position in front of the telly.

Drinking his cocoa, Grandpa Joe listened intently at the news, with the volume turned up. He absorbed the facts like a sponge and would always form concrete ideas on issues of the day, especially relating to trade unions and the working class, recounting the details of these subjects over the next few days and constructing his own arguments with those he met daily in the village.

He watched as the Prime Minister of the time, Harold Wilson, once more came to stay in his holiday cottage on the Isles of Scilly, thinking to himself that this would be the nearest he would ever be to anyone from London coming down here. But this turned out to be far from the truth, as one day a letter arrived stating that he had been recommended for a long time service award for working on the same farm for over fifty years.

Grandpa Jo meets Prince Charles

This was to be presented by Prince Charles at the Royal Cornwall Show.

It was June 1970, the time of the year for this prestigious event to take place.

But it wasn't just special for Cornwall. The Thomas family was full with great excitement as the day arrived and Grandpa Joe got himself spruced up looking proper fine in his smart suit and tie as we all set off for the show at Wadebridge.

In nervous anticipation we watched as he took his place in line with all the other veterans sharing this occasion, and wondered to ourselves what he might say to the prince.

'Congratulations Mr Thomas on achieving this prodigious award, you look very well. But if you are over 80, how old is your employer?' asked the prince.

'About the same age, sir,' he replied. 'I've worked for the same family all this time!'

We held our breaths!

'Well yes… hard work never killed anyone did it, sir?' he replied to the prince.

They shook hands and his moment of fame was over. We were all very proud of him on that day; he was in his eighties by then, but he appeared to thoroughly enjoy the day out and of course used it as the main topic of conversation with his 'ladies' and the codgers at Boat Cove for many months to come.

Grandpa Joe receives his Long Service Award from Prince Charles at the Royal Cornwall Show in the 1960's   (I am circled in the background)

As Grandpa Joe was the main authority on most topics of general knowledge, I asked him one day how I might make the ginger beer, I was nurturing in a saucer, a bit stronger.

In my childhood we used to share around the village a ginger beer plant that you cultivated in a saucer, adding water, sugar and ginger extract to it to enhance the taste and saving this in a bottle for future use. Everyone would have their chance to produce the best tasting ginger beer and the bottle with the biggest kick was acknowledged the best in the village.

My Grandpa advised me to give it extra sugar and ginger to give it some bite, so this is what we did. We could watch it growing and fizzing daily; then the tasting day arrived and sure enough it certainly had a vicious bite to it.

'Enough to blow your socks off!' declared Grandpa Joe as he consumed his fair share and we all agreed his part in the recipe added more than a kick to our sample.

The Butt Making Competition

The long summer holidays from school had arrived. By the time we were halfway through we started to get bored and this was one of those days. Lyn Laity, Elizabeth Perfect, John Sewell and myself were wondering what to do to occupy our time when we passed Grandpa Joe in the road.

'What you lot up to then?' he asked.

None of us really gave him an answer, more like a long moaning sound.

'Want something to make?' he suggested.

'Oh yes!' came a loud chorus of replies.

We all followed him to his work shed, which was a little hut on the edge of his field of violets, and there in the corner was a set of wheels that had been taken off an old pram. He picked them up and showed us.

'Know what you can do with these do you?' he asked, his eyes twinkling.

Most of us had no idea, but from his expression we reckoned we were in for a bit of a treat.

'You can make a fine 'butt' with this pair,' he murmured.

He then pulled out an array of different lengths of wood from behind his bench, and placed them in front of us.

'See you put this bit here, add this, fix the wheels, add a steering wheel and you're made. Go on give it a try.'

So furiously we all set to work and in no time at all the shed was full with many bits and pieces including several wheels, so we started up a competition to see who could make the best 'butt'; we all frantically hammered and glued for days until something like a couple of 'butts' were taking shape.

Finally the planks of wood were laid, the steering wheels and eight wheels were in place, and none too close to the ground. We had made them wide and long enough so that four could easily fit it, one behind the other... Perfect.

We all looked at each other wondering what to do next. Then soon the idea came to mind, that we should have a race. We were to start off on the top of the hill by the church, down by where the Littlechilds lived and then swing around by the Perfects and carry on past our own cottage towards the farm, then zoom down to the beach.

We were going to find that the road here was only a sandy path, so that would finally help us come to a halt. Any afterthought was no good now. But a pair of brakes controlling the front and rear tyres wouldn't have come a miss; it was too late now anyway.

The day of the race arrived; we put extra sand at the finishing point so that we would be guaranteed to finish there, plus some bales of hay in case there was no other way to stop, for beyond this point there was a steep slope running down to the sea.

We assembled by the church and climbed aboard. Our two cousins, John and Paul, were at the front in charge of the controls of each butt and Grandpa Joe was getting ready to count us off from the starting point.

'Three, two, one... Go!' he shouted.

With an almighty heave using the soles of our shoes we all sped off, the person at the end giving the biggest push before he too jumped in with the rest, and we were off.

It was the best time of the day to be racing, because there were no cars to be found in the village and there was no chance of the cows sauntering along the village lane on their way to be milked. Anyway the cows were being turned out in the lush green fields right behind the farm at that moment, we had already checked with the farmer who lived there, so they didn't come out onto the lane at all.

The wind sang in our ears as we viewed the passing cottages that looked just like blurred images on the landscape; forever gaining speed and squealing at the top of our voices as we manoeuvred the bends, we swayed around the few corners and nearly fell out of our 'butts' as we were pulled from side to side.

All too soon we were on the last lap of our adventure, the road from the farmhouse and down to the top of the beach. We were neck and neck in our race, scraping each other's sides as each surged forward, trying to be first to the winning post and coming to a full stop, we prayed, in the bales of hay we had planted earlier.

As this came into view all went blank; the noise, the screaming came to a stop, the speed all became one as we thumped into the wall of hay and sand. Then all that was visible was everyone's back ends as 'butt', children and sand muffled the cries of the desperate in their attempt to escape, and already Grandpa Joe was running to the scene as fast as his old legs could carry him.

Chapter Five
SAFFRON BUNS AT ST IVES

Sunday School Tea-treat in the 1960s

Sundays were special days in our Methodist household when I was growing up. All family members were dressed in their 'Sunday best' and attended chapel twice that day. But this strict regime reaped some rewards; for example we received Sunday School prizes for good attendance every year. I can remember on one occasion, I felt very proud of receiving my reward of copies of *Heidi* and *Treasure Island*.

I read them over and over again as sacred pieces and they nurtured my love of stories from an early age.

The other highlight of our Christian year was the annual Sunday School Tea-treat. It was not some vast museum visit in the heart of a city centre. Instead we boarded a train from Lelant to St Ives, armed with our baskets full of huge saffron buns and glass bottles of Corona, all set for a day on the beach.

With trepidation we would open the bedroom curtains early on the morning of the great day, keeping our fingers crossed that the weather would be good so that we could wear our best outfits.

Mum would pack our bag for the day with swimming costumes, swimming hats, extra underwear and a towel each, plus our brand new buckets and spades.

We would all get ushered down to the village green where all would gather for the great occasion. There waiting for us would be a Primrose coach all booked to take us to Lelant station, which in reality was only a few miles from St Ives, but the excitement of where this train journey was going to take us was enough to make us vow to attend Sunday School until the end of our days, if we had to, in order to experience this adventure.

We had a fairly big party of children for these occasions, many of whom might make their excuses not to come to Sunday services once in a while, but the treat to the beach was a date firmly stamped in our memory.

We had two leaders who took us: they were Marjorie Thomas, known to all of us as 'Aunty Marjorie' and Cyril Andrews, who was a local preacher as well as the circuit steward for our chapel.

For most of the time the children were well behaved; of course we would never dream of being naughty as we viewed this occasion as a real treat and besides the last thing our parents had said to us was, 'Now you behave yourselves and have a lovely day' and that is exactly what everyone wanted and did.

As we boarded the coach and vied for the seat near the window, all would settle down with a contented air that we were now on our way. Cheers would go up as we waved to anxious parents standing on the green, followed by a few jeers from the older members as the Primrose coach struggled to complete its short journey to the station. But these were soon lost in the echoes of our voices singing, 'Ten green bottles' as the holiday atmosphere descended on the gathering.

As we turned into the railway station, we could see the train arriving with its billows of smoke rising up into the sky and forming little clouds above our heads. The train appeared like a great heaving monster as we waited patiently for our turn to board it. Through clouds of steam that fogged our view inside we again all jostled for the best seats inside the carriages. No sooner had we sat down than we heard the sound of the stationmaster outside, as he checked the doors were all shut before blowing his whistle, giving the all clear to depart.

The first jolt of the train lurched us forward and we were on our way. It purred and hooted its way along the track, then with the final descent into St Ives, the carriage was suddenly filled with the sound of excited shouts from all of us. 'I can see the beach, look at all that blue water.'

The twisted journey downwards to the edge of the shore filled us with excitement. Finally the train stopped adjacent to the beach and we all tumbled out, ready to invade the golden sands below.

'Right find your partners and hold hands,' Cyril and Marjorie told us.

They picked up the baskets full of goodies for our lunch and we all trooped off towards the waiting sand and sea. The first thing on our minds was to feel the warmth of that sand between our toes and then head straight for the water.

The air was filled with the intoxicating smell of the sea inviting us to join its swirling foaming tide. We discarded our shoes as we made a bee-line for the sea, trails of hastily pulled off clothes following each youngster, as all of us jumped and tumbled into the water.

Our invasion of the beach would be reinforced as we established our pitch in the sunniest, brightest corner, taking over a fair proportion of the beach.

So after that first cold dipping of the toes in the water, we all jumped in and enjoyed our long awaited swim, before we went back to base camp to feast on the treats that waited for us.

Dripping wet, shivering, with damp towels wrapped around our shoulders, we returned and sat quietly waiting for the saffron buns. Our wet hands politely acknowledged the acceptance of this gift to each Sunday School member, and then we tucked into the large soft doughy circles of sheer pleasure. As we bit into them the tangy saffron spice would tingle the taste buds and we would chew away on the currants and sultanas as if we had never tasted the likes of it before.

With renewed energy it was back to the water. After our swim we held competitions to see who could build the biggest sandcastle and then, if the tide was on the turn, we would choose a spot a few yards from the edge and dig down deep to build the biggest boat ever; carving the sand to make a sharp bow and seats with a high side, we would then all huddle down in its depths, confident we would be safe in its confines as the sea invaded the shore and spilled over the top of our magnificent sand-crafted boat.

Certainly there were many activities that kept us busy during this precious outing. Then before we knew it, it was time to rub the sand off, wash our feet and get dressed again. All the belongings were packed away and wearily our happy band of pilgrims trudged over to the station and boarded the train home.

Singing might be started by a few, but inevitably most of us just curled up and gave in to those drooping eyelids until we reached our destination.

Then totally happy but extremely exhausted we would be helped home to sleep off the effects of the day, hoping that tomorrow was not a Sunday, so we didn't have to get up early to go to chapel.

Chapter Six
TOO POSH TO PEE IN A (CHAMBER) POT?

My sister and brother and I thought life was especially hard for us each summer, as our household was turned upside-down and drastically re-arranged as we prepared for the summer season.

Taking in visitors in our tiny cottage was a feat beyond imagination in those days. My brother being a deep sea fisherman would sometimes come home and his bedroom had some trippers staying in it, so his bedroom was a tent in the garden.

In this day and age we certainly would not have satisfied any of the stringent health and safety regulations that apply today.

We had no bathroom; the loo was at the end of the garden and washing consisted of a strip wash delicately done using the contents of what would fit into the china bowl set strategically placed in each bedroom.

Water for this operation had to be heated from a tiny heater over the kitchen sink and carefully carried up to the bedroom when required. We only had three bedrooms for us all to live in – mum and dad slept downstairs on a 'put you up' that had a great metal mechanism that pulled out from the wall, in the area that was our only private place, where we ate and gathered together.

That left mum and dad's bedroom free as the only double bedroom, which also fitted another single bed as well. My sister and I were squashed into the middle room with our two beds crammed together so there was no spare room; we had all the contents of my parents' bedroom, our wardrobe and two chests of drawers with all the things we would need for the duration of the summer months packed around us, so there was absolutely nowhere to move.

Life was certainly hectic, as my sister was working she was out most of the time but she had a local boyfriend who would usually turn up for evening meals just as it was being served and be one more to cater for. I was left to be chief washer-upper, waitress and chambermaid to my mum.

As we lived in a farmworker's tied cottage my mum had to ask permission from the farmer to take in visitors in the summer. This helped to supplement my dad's wages that were very low and again we worked as a family in this.

My mum and I would set off for the violet fields early on the Saturday mornings armed with our violet picking baskets and dressed against the cold. All the little blue flowers had to be delicately picked with a strong stem so that they made a strong bunch altogether.

All had to be counted into piles and placed in the pathway by the side so that Grandpa Joe following behind could gather them up and estimate the number of leaves needed each time.

It was back-breaking work, then they all had to be sorted and bunched into 15 blue flowers all looking the same way with two leaves and packed ready for market.

Summers were much more fun. For the Band B business we would put up a sign at the end of the garden advertising ourselves to the people who would be passing by on their way to the beach.

We charged £1.2 shillings and sixpence, with children being ten shillings (50p in today's money) nightly which rose an extra 5 shillings if evening meal was included.

We saw all sorts through our doors; one scruffy English teacher brought a group of pupils down for a cricket tournament and found himself sleeping in his car in the car park.

My dad rescued him from here and brought him home for the night, even though he was unable to cover the cost of the accommodation. Soon after this chap gave up teaching and turned to his first love of painting and became famous in the Midlands for his work.

John Stubbs was commissioned by Marks & Spencer for his countryside scenes on Christmas cards and calendars, which now have been used on tapestries and embroidery work as well. His family regularly returned to us and he painted my mum a lovely seascape for her 50th birthday when they were with us.

We had another couple on their honeymoon who thought it would be especially nice to return home with a lovely Cornish tan; to enhance this they used pure coconut oil all over their bodies and ended up in casualty with sunstroke.

They couldn't bear to go near each other for a cuddle and by the time they were ready to go home they looked like native Red Indians with peeling skins.

Another young girl was totally fed up when the first week of her much looked-forward-to holiday was a total wash out. As soon as the sun came out on the morning of her second week she took off to the beach; she sunbathed all day till the sun went down and then returned back stiff and sore.

My mum, on seeing her return from the beach, made a jug full of ice cold milk mixed with bicarbonate of soda which she applied to the skin in the form of a sticky paste; this was like an all-over facemask but certainly eased the burning of the sunburn.

We also had a run of folk singers who came to Cornwall to take in the local folk scene popular in the 1960s, and consequently filled our sitting room with the locals and trippers. We all took part in loud singsongs on hot summer evenings, where neighbours and friends could be found sitting on the stairs, in the hallway and in the doorways in their enthusiasm to join in.

At Trewellard near Pendeen, a chapel was converted into the so-called Piper's Folk Club at this time, where I sat next to a rather nervous Ralph McTell as he prepared to sing with the late, great Brenda Wootton.

We had our folk singers staying with us; it was during the sixties when the whole world luxuriated in 'peace and love'.

Songs were echoing to the strains of 'if you're going to San Francisco... be sure to wear some flowers in your hair' and everyone was being urged to 'make love and not war'.

On a more local level the seafront in St Ives was swarming with 'beatniks' many of whom had come from the cities down to Cornwall to let it all hang loose there.

The Piper's Folk Club

It was an era when Sandy Shaw chose to sing, 'Puppet on a String' wearing no shoes and scantily-clothed layabouts would hang out in the harbour in St Ives proclaiming free love to all, getting free food if they could and having a great time.

Some of them found their way over to our coast and beach, bringing with them their music and songs. These were some of the 'folky' type that filled our folk clubs.

Luckily the lighting in the folk club was subtle so that hidden corners were quite dark so it was not unusual to spy, during a serious singing session, a spider or two or some other member of the crawling kind lazily making its way across the stage during a performance.

I am grateful that I never had the chance to inspect such premises as these during daylight hours as I think we would have had to admit that we were only visitors sharing the animals' habitat for a few hours.

In the hot summer months when we couldn't move for trippers it was packed full of singers. The former pews had been taken out and there was a space in the middle cleared for acts to perform.

Nets were slung across its beams and fishing memorabilia were decorating the huge windowsills, giving it a distinct fishy atmosphere. Most of the lighting was by candles, which generated monstrous shadows in its murky interior and further added to its unique setting.

Heaven knows what health and safety would have made of it today; we just sat around all on the same level, on benches and barrels and dutifully joined in with the various performances.

One well-known act at the time was a certain Jasper Carrott – with hair – who could play the guitar well, and would sing with his reasonable gritty voice songs from his native North.

Brenda Wootton, who wore great flowing kaftans and was accompanied by her soul mate, John the Fish, sang very lovely and sweetly. This lady turned out to be an ambassador for Cornwall, taking our songs to Brittany and beyond in the name of her county.

She was a lovely person and indeed personified the Cornish folk scene with her hard work during this time. During an age in which we made our own entertainment, this was on a par with such programmes today as, *Britain's Got Talent* only, we made up the live music where everyone joined in and a great time was guaranteed to be had by all.

The Count House at St Just was another centre for such entertainment: a converted wooden shed in the grounds of a big house. But gradually, as in any situation where there might be a free for all with few rules and no discipline the red tape and those in command declared such meetings might not be too safe so the whole scene was moved to The Western Hotel in Penzance.

With this came the introduction of a bar, comfortable seats and microphones and the whole country ambience was lost forever.

In the 1970s I was singing 'Streets of London' to my mates at college – who always thought me to be a 'bit thick' coming from Cornwall, yet when this song became No.1 in the charts they quickly changed their minds and I found myself very popular in the summer holidays when a break in Cornwall didn't seem such a bad thing after all.

Chris Rowe and Ian Clark, Folk singers from Hull who stayed with us in the 1960's

England Win the World Cup 1966

It was the summer of 1966 that saw the most memorable event in our sitting room. This was special for most people in this country as England played Germany in the World Cup and everyone would be familiar with where they were at that special moment when England scored, being ingrained on the mind like recalling the dreadful moment when Kennedy or Elvis died.

At this time, being mid-August, we had a houseful of people as usual, who were always being told off for not being present when the evening meal was due to be served. They were inevitably in the local pub; but this day was quite different.

These trippers, our guests, found some Germans in the pub and thought it would be interesting if they too crowded into the room to watch the match.

As we were favoured with one of the few television sets in the village, our sitting room began filling for this occasion well in advance of kick-off time. The television was perched at the highest vantage point in the room with every available chair placed in its wake.

Yorkshireman and German sat side-by-side, making the atmosphere very sweaty and volatile for all watching. We had two big mats on the floor on top of the carpets which mum said helped its general wear and tear and these were stretched out near the door so that all could be catered for.

We had all the doors and windows open and anyone passing and learning of the event just wandered in. Although the event could only be seen in black and white, the atmosphere was blue, in fact I got sent out of the room at one stage because the language was so bad, but I still listened from outside.

The surges of amazement and desolation from the audience were wafted along on the air as the ball was passed from end to end; many were convinced that the Ref must have been totally blind as the ball was passed along the German line, then deafening applause, whistling and cheering as England tackled and thrust and proceeded to the goal to finish on those infamous words, 'They think its all over – it is now.'

In one death defying crescendo the English realised that for once they had won something and then the flopped back into reality.

The group sitting on the mat near the door looked down to see that they had moved right over to the doorstep in their excitement. The Germans were immediately deflated exclaiming that they would beat the English next year and the Yorkshiremen declared arrogantly that they thought the English would have won anyway – no contest – so with good will on both sides all declared this was a time for celebration and they wandered off to see if the pub had opened yet.

They all left with a stern warning from my mum ringing in their ears – that they had better make sure they were back for seven, as dinner would be on the table as usual at that time and anyone who was not there would go without.

Other visitors who came through our doors

It was me who happened to open the door that day and I was confronted by a very pretty woman, who was wearing lots of make-up like my sister did, but this was applied just right so that it enhanced her cheek bones and showed off her blonde hair style to its full extent, which was piled high on the top of her head, giving the whole halo effect; indeed with the sun shining behind her she looked like an angel or least a goddess standing there. I was mesmerised.

She asked me very politely if my mother was in, but she had left a short while before. Upon my answer of no, she asked me if we had any vacant rooms; as it was a Saturday I knew we were free again for the coming week and mum and I had already changed the beds that morning in preparation for any new visitors.

Mum had gone with dad to do shopping and left me in charge and I knew the routine off by heart. So when I told her there were rooms available, she clapped her hands with glee and said this was just what she and her husband were looking for.

I thought she exaggerated her happiness with a lot of smiling and posh words like, 'how quaint' and 'marvellous' and seemed to be a bit confused as to how to go on. Anyway she took command and said she would return with her husband a little later. 'Will an hour be OK miss?' she asked.

I told her that would be fine and added 'bye for now', but when I closed the door I felt as if she had taken my breath away.

When mum returned I recounted the arrival of our latest visitor and she seemed a bit mystified, not being really sure how they might fit in.

An hour later this lady called Mavis and her husband John were sitting in our front room drinking tea from the best china. mum was putting on a show and having this quiet ordinary conversation about Cornish life!

'This seems exactly what we were looking for isn't it love?' the woman enthused to her husband, who was, in comparison to her quite quiet and serious, being tall and skinny with a neat beard and long artistic fingers.

Mum showed them to the best room we had; it was large and sunny they loved it.

Mum said she would bring up some hot water so that they might wash before their evening meal and if they wanted the loo it was at the end of the garden, but there was a chamber pot under the bed if they were caught short!

There were squeals of laughter from their room as John brought in their many suitcases and lugged them up the stairs. As mum and I were preparing the evening meal, there was much activity from their room and they emerged later looking very fine.

Mavis was in a lilac trouser suit with very high stilettos and looked even prettier than a few hours before and John was in a blazer and light trousers and sandals. um had bought out all the best china and had pulled out all the stops to provide a sumptuous meal for these two; it was a lovely, mouth-watering roast and tasted as delicious as it had smelled when cooking. Yet it was her Cornish pasties that were to die for. She made them so scrumptious and so big that they used to hang over the edge of the plates when presented to our guests.

My mum was certainly a very good cook, making do in a tiny kitchen which was long and narrow, being hardly big enough for one working, let alone two preparing dishes, and she always cooked extra so that we could sit down and eat ours when the paying guests had had theirs.

Meal times were hectic for a short time, then peace descended as we all ate. It was usually my job to attack the washing up; this would all be neatly piled up in order on the draining board so that things were kept tidy at all times. Plates from the main course were rinsed off first ready to have a thorough wash later.

Then we got the saucepans out of the way so that we had more room for everything else, then clean water again before we really started the wash.

Glasses were washed first of course, then the sweet dishes because they weren't very dirty, then the dinner plates again and last of all the cutlery.

Dad would do the wiping of the dishes and mum would put away. In no time at all we would be back to normal and then ready for coffee at the end of the meal. We might join our guests in the other room and have an informal chat with them to end off the evening.

All this was done using the only source of hot water we had, which was a tiny water heater above the sink and this was the only space where we ourselves could get washed and dressed when we had a full house. I don't know how any of us got through this time, but we did and enjoyed it too.

Mavis and John had a lovely week with us; they were gone all day in the lovely weather. Mavis always took ages to get ready to go out but always looked immaculate in her dress and make-up. John would get very irritated with the time she took in this preparation and would be ready in minutes and then wander through to our kitchen to have a chat with us.

Then the weather changed to rain so they stayed in a bit more. There were no rules in the house for guests to vacate their rooms at any set time so we would usually end up all sitting round in the front room talking on wet days. However on this particular day the weather deteriorated during the day until there was a howling gale by night-time.

Mavis on this occasion needed to go to the loo, but on opening the front door found the wind right in her face. We begged her to hang on until the wind died down, but she was desperate. Stilettos were changed for rubber boots; the designer top was swapped for a yellow southwester and the battle against the elements began.

The path to the loo was long and arduous and slippery and your reward on reaching its comfort was a draughty, dimly lit enclosure that you shared with the spiders.

Some time later Mavis battled back up the path with straggly hair, water dripping from her face and her boots covered in mud, to be greeted with rapturous applause from us all gathered in the doorway ready with hot chocolate as a reward for this feat.

When she had been dried off and her hands brought back to life, she declared meekly that there was no way she would attempt such a journey in those conditions again, declaring to all that next time she would use the chamber pot under the bed like the rest of us. Blue skies and hot sun returned the next day, however and all declarations were forgotten like those made during the howling gale of the previous night, never to be mentioned again.

Mavis and John emerged immaculately dressed in the morning, although the stilettos had now been replaced with flatter shoes but the make-up was as flawless as ever and remained so for the next thirty years they visited us. They became our good friends.

On the occasion of my mum's fiftieth birthday in 1971 Mavis and John were still visiting us regularly, Mavis as perfect as ever. John was being secretive but it turned out that he was now an accomplished artist, being commissioned by a nationwide firm for his calendars and Christmas cards. They would disappear for hours walking along the cliffs and yes he was busy painting the lovely scenes along the way. At the end of this holiday he tiptoed up to their room after the evening meal then called us all into the dining room, where low and behold he unveiled the most glorious painting of a beach scene he'd done just around the corner from the main beach.

This was mum's birthday present and a really fitting thank you to us all for the many years they had visited us and the many happy hours they had enjoyed in Cornwall.

Chapter Seven
THE DAY THE OIL CAME
[MARCH 18th 1967]

The Torrey Canyon

The most dramatic moment in the history of our beach came during the Easter of 1967. The drama began when the telephone rang and a senior member of the WRVS Service for West Penwith called to warn my mother that there was a major event in the area; a boat had been involved in an incident off the Scillies and was spilling its cargo of crude oil into the sea there. If the wind changed direction this oil would be blown onto our beaches. As my mother was a member of the WRVS (Woman's Royal Voluntary Service) she knew that her services would most likely be required soon.

We positioned ourselves in front of the radio and television hoping to glean some news of the event; we didn't have long to wait.

The boat was called the *Torrey Canyon,* a bulk oil carrier, and she was sailing for Milford Haven with 120,000 tons of Kuwait oil. It had run aground on Pollard Rock on the Seven Stones Reef off Land's End, through the negligence of the master of the boat.

Thirty thousand gallons of oil had escaped and was being moved steadily towards the Cornish coast by the prevailing winds and currents. Prime Minister Harold Wilson spoke to the nation of his concern for the Cornish coastline.

All attempts to move or break the boat up failed. The latest suggestion at the time was to burn the oil surrounding the stricken vessel.

As soon as the Monday after the weekend of the disaster came the full extent of the damage was becoming clear. The Royal Air Force and the Royal Navy implemented an early warning system for the oil movement.

The oil was to be sprayed with emulsifier to break it up as fast as possible; there were now 18 RN vessels assigned to this, with plans to increase these numbers each day as the oil spread in different directions.

The coastguard at Lands End confirmed our wildest fears that the oil was moving closer and closer to Sennen beach and the surrounding coast, but there was nothing anyone could do.

The government were full of good ideas; such as erecting boons across the bays to stop the mess coming ashore and putting barriers up on the beaches as the silent slick moved inwards, but in the end nothing could stop the sludgy mess from coming ashore.

It was the smell that was the worst!

It crept in through the windows as we slept and down through the chimney and under the floor; it clogged your nostrils, your mouth and made your eyes smart, but the good news was that local authorities were to be helped in the clean up operations by the introduction of troops to the worst areas.

We all visited the beach daily, like detectives looking for signs of the foreign invader. At first it began with small puddles and splodges, but gradually the tide turned into a chocolate custard whirling the stuff in all directions. Then the fateful day arrived.

The smell had got stronger so we knew the full invasion had begun and we needed to get down to the beach to view the chaos for ourselves.

Dad put on his oilers and boots and we set off to survey the beach. When we got there it looked like a war scene; in fact if this had been a scene from the ravages of war, our beach would have been described as receiving a 'direct hit' making it unrecognisable, as though someone from above had poured thick gravy over the whole place.

There was no sand visible but in the covering we could see movement as if from under a blanket. We were instructed to stay by the steps while my dad observed. He thought he saw something moving a little way out and he was right; there in the centre of the beach was a beak attached to a head squiggling desperately to get free of the oil and a faintly flapping wing.

Dad attempted to cover a few yards across the sand but the oil was so deep it came in over his boots, so he was forced to turn back, leaving the poor bird to fight for his life.

It was decided that spraying the affected beaches with detergent might help as a first step in the clear-up operations. So over the next few days and weeks farmers forwarded their spraying equipment that they used on their crops as apparatus for the scheme, and other spraying equipment was modified as well.

The blowing up of the Torrey Canyon

During the next few days the troops were beginning to turn up by the lorry full and our village was turned into what looked like a war zone. The car park was full with all the barrels of detergent and on the main road the Easter Weekend traffic was brought to a standstill as even more lorries were rushed to the coast with the treasured barrels.

The troops came from all ranks and areas of the British Isles. They appeared to be very young and handsome to our young eyes, being thirteen at this time; so, whenever a young soldier walked by we would of course get a fit of the giggles. But the realism of the situation on the beach, where there was no sand to be seen at all, seemed to put our romantic thoughts about the young troops to one side.

The troops had no choice but to attack the enemy head on; with great determination they took deep breaths and courageously tried to walk through this choking quagmire. The oil was like a quicksand reaching out to pull all around into its consuming chasm.

We were banned from the beaches so most days we were told to stay upon the cliffs and view the scene from there. Our job became watching out for bird movement under the chocolate canopy and shouting out their positions to the men below.

Then the troops armed in their thick overalls and gloves could move forward and explore the quivering heaps that were silently screaming to be rescued from their nightmare and be given some air. Yet what air was there to breathe? It was toxic and thick with oil, this smell penetrating into all unprotected orifices.

Specialised hospital volunteers were working around the clock to deal with hundreds of birds that had been brought to them at the Mousehole Bird Sanctuary. Traditional treatments that had been successful in the past seemed to have little effect on the poor injured birds now and many died. When we took our baskets of dying birds to the sanctuary which people had left along the road, the place was so full.

Not only did the birds suffer but the volunteers suffered headaches, stomach upsets and burns as they applied different solutions to the birds.

Many volunteers turned up showing eagerness to take part. Bankers worked alongside farm hands and any idea of class was forgotten as the one common aim was to free the beaches of oil.

In Britain the help that was sent to us in the form of the armed services totalled 1.400 personnel. These troops suffered from streaming eyes from the detergent, and romantic ideas that the young ladies of the village might have connected with these young lads was reduced to intense pity for them, as they poured into the WRVS centre to have their eyes bathed and bandaged before resting for a short period before returning to the scene.

After the beaches were clean there was the small isolated coves to be cleared of oil, so the soldiers had to climb down the cliffs to get to them, having to put up with bruised knees and cut ankles caused by the jagged rocks they had to climb.

So the conclusion of this massive disaster was that the Torrey Canyon was blown up by Sea Vixens and Buccaneers from the navel stations of Yeovilton and Culdrose, followed by R.A.F. Hunters with a supply of napalm to ignite the oil. Gradually the oil relented and so did the troops and the chocolate sludge was replaced by green/blue waves lapping gently on our shores.

The captain of the tanker was held to be solely responsible for the grounding of his ship. Having to live with the terrible consequences of that day was punishment enough for anybody.

Today we still have the same dawn chorus of wild birds waking us up as soon as the sun rises on summer mornings, and the vast amounts of seagulls still continue to be a nuisance in our coastal towns, but we should be continually thankful that we still have many of them with us, considering the great disaster we went through on that Easter weekend of 1967.

Mum (far left) with members of the W.R.S and an Officer who worked on the Torrey Canyon Oil Spill 1967

Chapter Eight
CAROLYN'S WEDDING

Grandpa Joe, Carolyn and Grandpa Issac

My Sister's Wedding 1968

Grandpa Joe was in so much trouble; Aunty Muriel was making the bridesmaids' dresses for my sister's wedding and disaster struck... the heaters in the house were empty so Grandpa Joe brought the big can of paraffin in to fill them.

Unknown to him the container had a hole in the bottom so on the way to the heaters the paraffin leaked all over the turquoise, velvet bridesmaid dresses.

I have never seen Aunty Muriel so mad... Grandpa Joe made a hasty exit and sought refuge at our house for a while too afraid to go home.

The dresses were soaked in the bath and washed several times until eventually the marks all came out; they were beautiful and what complemented them was the twenty-five velvet-covered buttons down the back. Although they took ages to get into they looked perfect. After all the drama it was an ideal wedding.

We all knew that my sister would marry the man of her dreams because as he brought her home from work each evening on the back of his motorbike, he would be singing, 'Peek a boo I love you, you're the one girl for me.'

He was blessed with a lovely voice and good looks. My mum loved it when he sang 'Old Tige', her favourite Jim Reeves song.

What can you say about my sister, Carolyn. She couldn't settle at anything. After leaving school her first job was as a machinist in St Ives, but found she couldn't get on with the girls there. She didn't stay there long and got a job in our local post office which had a small shop with Mrs Crothers and her husband George. She liked this a lot and got on well but eventually got itchy feet and thought she could get more money working in the local cinema in Penzance. At one time, during a promotion for the Beatles film *Help*, the staff were given dresses signed by the Famous Four but hers got thrown away when we moved house, which infuriated her, as today it would be worth a fortune!

This was her job when she got married in 1968. Ken, her husband-to-be, lived in St Buryan. He worked as a farmhand and would pick her up after work and bring her home, then stay for a while and have a meal with us.

Plans were being made for the wedding and it was decided that Carolyn would get married on 9 March at

Perranuthnoe Church. The weather was good for the time of year and all the village turned out to watch.

Carolyn, walking with dad, followed by me and Lyn Laity to the church, 1968

Of course I was one of the bridesmaids; Lyn my friend, and my cousin Helen Newton on our side and two on the groom's side made up the rest. To complement the infamous velvet dresses we had to wear matching Dutch-type bonnets, which my sister thought looked the part. Lyn and I being in our early teens felt quite embarrassed by them, but Carolyn knew this and said we had no choice in the matter, so that was it.

Even so the day went off well. There was quite a nip in the air on the day so the church heaters were turned on beforehand, everyone was present and we were in our places, when, while the blessing was taking place I suddenly heard a rustling behind me. Glancing back I saw the page boy undressing himself. The poor little chap had ended up being placed right next to one of the heaters and had became too hot. I rushed back to help him get redressed before the prayer was over and the congregation opened their eyes again. The mother of the boy yanked him back to help to finish the job in hand, just in time before we made our exit from the church.

Needless to say, by the time we had all gathered in the vicarage garden for the photos this four-year-old was immaculately dressed again. We all travelled into town to have the reception in a posh hotel there and the happy couple had their photos taken on the promenade with the sea as their backdrop.

Ken's job took them to live in a farm cottage near St Austell which was old-fashioned but cosy, and very soon after this they began their family. Their first born was Andrew and, the first grandchild in the family, he was very welcomed by all and quite spoilt.

Mum spent a lot of time at their house which was a three-hour trip on the bus. Not long after came a little girl, Joanne. At this time in her life, Carolyn seemed to be at her most contented, being a young mother bringing up her young family with help not too far away if she needed it.

Chapter Nine
THE SCHOOL CRUISE

On reflection, I wondered how my parents paid for this wedding because during the next year I was allowed to go on a Mediterranean cruise with my school on the *S.S. Uganda*. I was fifteen by this time and remember bringing the papers back from school and leaving them on the kitchen table in the hope my parents might see them there.

The prospect of going on a big ship from Falmouth appealed to me very much. Perhaps I had some sea blood in my veins similar to my brother. The cost was £45 and we would be visiting Ceuta and Teutan on the North African coast, as well as stopping off in Gibraltar, Corsica, Pisa and Florence. The idea of seeing all those countries was mind-blowing; thinking that this might be possible from Cornwall, seemed so out of reach.

Imagine my surprise when my parents actually agreed to me going. The trip was all planned and we were to go with my headmaster and my R E teacher. As I was the eldest in our group my headmaster decided to put me in charge of five of the younger ones.

This meant that we all shared a dormitory together so I had to stop them arguing over who would sleep in the top bunk or the bottom, and set them certain tasks to keep the room spotless. We had competitions with the other schools who were with us to see who were the best in these things.

Therefore, every morning, we all gathered together to judge the cleanest sink, loo, floor and best-made beds. This was all very well until we came through the Bay of Biscay when the weather couldn't have got any worse.

In the canteen, plates, cups, saucers and cutlery rushed from one side of the tables to the other, but no one cared at this point though; food was the last thing on their minds as most of them were too busy throwing up the remains of their last meal.

I felt a bit queasy but once I got into the rhythm of the swaying from side to side and up and down, I started to feel quite excited by it all.

Unfortunately, not many of my classmates felt the same way as me. Perhaps I was hardened to the affect of the rough weather by the times I had crossed to the Scillies on the *Scillionian* when I was young. I don't know but like all new experiences in my life, I enjoyed this one.

What got me through this was that I went up on deck and let the spray of the sea splash my face I could then relax, with the motion of the ship as she was battered in all directions. Not once did I feel unsafe.

Once through this rough patch things immediately began to improve. Our first port of call was the island of Corsica. It was where Napoleon had spent some time and everywhere we went we were reminded of this. It made me remember when we all went to Stratford Upon Avon and it was all centred around Shakespeare. But we did experience some light relief here in the form of our headmaster demonstrating to us how to use the French loos. Anyone familiar with this culture knows that you have to squat down over a hole to relieve yourself. I think I just held on until we got back on board the ship.

Our Headmaster was an oldish man called Mr James. His nickname was 'Jessie James' yet anything more unlike a Western cowboy would be hard to find. He certainly made hard work of this demonstration and had us all in fits of laughing as some attempted to follow his example.

Even so, Corsica was pretty and pleasantly hot so we had a good time here. Then we moved on to Italy. Our first stop was Pisa. I had read all about this leaning tower but I was quite disappointed when we were directed to the field where it stood.

Apparently the experts had discovered that it was sinking into the ground and the leaning was approaching a worrying angle. Therefore they were trying to reinforce the tilting so it was covered in scaffolding to keep it up.

I had visions of climbing up here but that proved impossible on the day so we just took photos, bought mementos and left. The next stop was much more interesting.

This was Florence. We viewed the Baptist doors of brass next to the cathedral that displayed scenes from the Bible, then moved on to the Uffizi Art Gallery, where I encountered some of the original works by Michelangelo, Van Gough and other Italian artists.

I thought the whole trip had been worthwhile; although I don't acknowledge myself as being an artistic kind of person, I couldn't help but be amazed at some of these paintings that looked as though, if you just blinked for a second, the scene would come to life before your eyes.

After Italy we made our way back to North Africa. Here it was unbearably hot and the place was full of flies. Yet the culture was so different from the last country that it seemed like a place time had forgotten.

There was dust on or in everything. The people were so poor that you had the impression that they had only dressed in their gay, bright attire for our visit and once we had gone they would return to rags.

We stopped at a place where there were camels for us to ride and a toothy black man forced a snake around my neck while my friends took photos of me. This wasn't so bad as the ride on the camel I agreed to. Talk about this creature being the 'ship of the desert', it was like the Bay of Biscay experienced all over again on dry land; and the camel constantly hissed at us and farted loudly for the duration of the short ride which made all watching curl up in embarrassment, and we still had more humiliation to come.

As we walked back to the boat along the quay the African traders hassled us to buy their goods and shouted out to us until we set foot safely on the boat again. To the sensitive teenage girls this was a harrowing experience.

The highlight of the trip was when we had a fancy dress party one night. Our dormitory decided to dress up as 'The Good, the Bad and the Ugly', which was a popular song at this time. Of course 'the Good' were the ones in the group who didn't feel like taking part and stayed in their school uniforms, just being themselves.

'The Bad' section were the rebellious ones who rarely conformed to anything like the rest of us did, so these were the ones wearing all the hideous make-up of the time, eyelashes like spiders peeping out and hair dyed all different colours.

'The Ugly' part of the group decided to be dressed as Arabs with their hissing, farting camels following on behind them. This turned out to be very funny, but unfortunately we lost out on a prize in the end to 'Sixties Pop Groups' who included the Beatles, The Rolling Stones and the Kinks, who mimed very well to popular music of the day.

Howard, Mum, George, Joslin, Albert & Betty (Taylor), Edna, Dad, Dorothy, Grandma, Grandpa, Ursula, Issac Reginald

Lasse Axel Axellson sister, Gun, all grown up

Bill, Me, Peter (who lives in New Zealand) & Sylvia August 2008

Family gathering on Perran Beach when mum made pasties for all 22 of us

Carolyn, Paul & Roger playing in the yard in the 1950's

My Family with the next generation of the Sewell family

Chapter Ten
SHE WAS ONLY THE FARMWORKER'S DAUGHTER

Green-acres Is The Place To Be: College Digs

My first choice for a college to attend was one in Coventry. This was the one where Paul Sewell, my cousin, had got into a few years before. Anyway I didn't get my first choice, which was nothing unusual, so it was to Worcester City that my mum and dad drove me all those years ago. When I knew that I had got a place here, the college fixed me up with digs for the first year so it was with a humble presence that we knocked on the door of 13 Green-acres Road, on one September day in 1972.

This was quite an impressive road, tree-lined and quiet. Immediately I loved the swishing of the trees and the leaves swirling down.

Carol and Ronnie Page were a young couple with two small sons. Their house was immaculate and when I was shown my room, I thought it was perfect and just right for studying.

I couldn't understand the way they spoke very well. They said they were 'Brummies' but I soon got used to the tilting, up and down sound of this. I was to be sharing with another girl who hadn't arrived yet so I knew that I'd have some company.

It was a tearful farewell as I waved mum and dad off for home again and really wished I was going back with them. I'd never been away from home before and knew it was a long journey back if I changed my mind.

My landlady and her husband were very kind and tried very hard to make me feel at home. They walked me down to college, which wasn't very far, and got me settled with the rest of my year group. They said it was better to walk to Worcester because they had a real problem with the traffic over Worcester Bridge, which I'd see on Monday morning.

Although I felt sad for many days, I eventually met a girl standing outside a study waiting to see the same personal tutor as me. Her name was Glenna Elliot. She lived at New Malden near London, seemed nice, and we had a few meals together in the canteen where I got to know her. Other friends came and joined our group: Elaine Best from Worthing, Sian Jones from Surrey, Pammie, Jennie and Barbara from Brum.

My first introduction to my room mate however was not so successful; she was brash and loud, and insisted on telling me the intimate details about her relationship with her boyfriend back in Bradford. These were things I just didn't want to hear. I suppose that I was a bit naïve and innocent which made me even more unhappy.

During my first days at college I didn't sleep or eat well and if it was not for the closeness of my newfound friends, or the sheer wonder at the college life that was going on around me, I think I would have asked to leave and rushed home to the security of my little Cornish home.

I also didn't like the course that I had decided to do, as the main subject I had chosen was RE. The students here seemed to be 'spaced out' on religion. When the Hare-Krishna group came into the building, chanting and waving their incense, I knew I couldn't go on.

Luckily I had a very sympathetic personal tutor who thought that perhaps I would be happier with a different main subject. I had chosen RE basically because I had a good result with it at 'A' level getting a B and also had a good knowledge of this in my own basic upbringing.

The only other choice I had was History because the English course was full, so I made the best of this but found it quite hard-going. Our tutors were near fanatics about Worcester and the English Civil War, but I didn't share their enthusiasm, so I made up for this when we did our own personal studies. Of course I chose something Cornish and studied Cornish Tin Mining in the Elizabethan era, bringing in the Stannary Parliaments and their working. The Stannary Parliaments were the local organisation of the tin mining culture in Cornwall at this time.

In the Scrum and the Birmingham bombings of the 1970s

My college days were generally great fun. One of the memorable moments was in the third year when we had the privilege of having our own rooms. Our group of best friends were all situated on the same floor so could meet up with each other when we wanted to.

The funniest moment came when we had a fire alarm in the early hours of one cold autumn morning. As it was generally rumoured that a fire drill was due, we were not particularly fazed when the alarm went off; it had only been a short time since we went to bed anyway.

I was so laid back that I put on extra clothing and refreshed my make-up, then went and knocked on my friend's door to see if she was ready to go down. As I stood there biding my time, it gradually dawned on me that my friend had already left and I was on my own.

All the males who were not allowed to stay overnight were rapidly getting down to the lower floors and jumping out of the back windows. Eventually I sauntered down and was the last one out. I swept past the waiting fireman to view the rest of our gang making eyes at them who, it turned out, had answered the 999 call only to find it was a false alarm.

But even so we had to remain in the car park until we had all been accounted for and the all clear had been given. The waiting boyfriends then dutifully got back in the windows and just carried on as before.

Teaching practice saw us all flung out in far parts of the Worcester and Shropshire countryside. As soon as I did my first one in Worcester City at a school called Gorse Hill, I knew that teaching was what I really wanted to do.

Perhaps it was something to do with the accommodating teacher I was with, a Mr Cooling. He was about to put on a musical called *Jonah Man Jazz* which I was able to play very well on my guitar, so I virtually took over this production and how proud I felt.

He even offered me a job at the school when I left college which would have suited me quite nicely but I was missing home and my ongoing boyfriend there who was thinking of asking me to get engaged soon, but it always made me think if I had accepted this position what might have happened if I had followed this path.

My subsequent teaching practise took me to Alverley, a remote school in the sticks of Shropshire, where to my annoyance the teacher who was expecting me was told to expect a boy call Julian!

He then asked that I do the internal workings of the combustion engine where his top juniors were studying the history of the car and was quite disappointed when I didn't quite get it.

It was all a bit sad here really because it was the time of the Black Panther in the Midlands and we were on strict curfew to be in before dark and then the doors were firmly locked and there was no going out after tea.

As it turned out this man called The Black Panther had kidnapped the heiress to a Midlands coach firm called Lesley Whittle and kept her down a drain asking for a ransom for her release. He wasn't caught in the time we were doing our teaching there and we tended to always be looking over our shoulders to see if we were being followed when we went back to our digs every night.

From here another of my postings was Bridgenorth in Shropshire. This was a beautiful market town with very friendly people, but I had a bad assessment when I couldn't for the life of me get round teaching fractions. Fortunately my tutor decided to stop the lesson and came back to assess me on a different subject which was hymn practice, my forte, so I passed the test.

College days were also overshadowed by bombings in Birmingham at this time. A lot of students were from Brum and had families at home so the bombing of the Bullring shopping centre left many frightened and shaken.

In our leisure activities we were always up for a laugh, especially playing rugby. All the girls in our gang – Glenna Elliott, Elaine Best, Sian Jones and Barbara Groves – thought we would make good hookers right in the middle of the scrum. So to make it more interesting we filled fairy liquid bottles with water, so that when we scrummed down we would get our opponents right in the face. What horrors we were, little but deadly.

I nearly failed passing out with my friends when the fateful day came for results. I was summoned for an interview and I knew my history knowledge left a lot to be desired. But on entering the tutors' rooms and being scared to death that all my three years had been in vain, they started to ask me about Cornwall: where I lived, what sort of place it might be for a holiday and if they might get a holiday on the cheap. I answered all of this in a positive way, offering holidays.

Surprisingly I passed through, but I was still an easy catch if anyone was looking for a cheap holiday in our neck of the woods. It was a matter not of what you might know, but of where you might live.

I missed home intensely; the sound of the sea had been replaced by trees swishing around me. Yet the next decision I took turned out to be not the best thing that I ever did. I got engaged to my Cornish boyfriend whom I didn't think I could live without. I soon lived to regret it.

Chapter Eleven
FIRST MARRIAGE AND
WHEN TEACHING WAS FUN

My First Teaching Post at Pendeen, near Land's End in the 1970s

Mrs Luxton! (Julia, Teacher), 1982

After I left College in the 1970s I was lucky to be accepted for the first post I applied for, leaving my fellow students at Worcester Teacher Training College and wishing each other well in the future.

Yet I believed that I was the only one who could boast that their new classroom had a sea view and also a working tin-mine in the village.

This area of Cornwall, the furthest south-west that was possible without falling into the sea at Land's End, was quite poor and the families were anything but affluent, yet the challenge of these children was exactly what I wanted.

Thus when I settled down with twenty-two seven-year-olds in the autumn of 1976 I hoped this might be all that I had ever wanted. I found it easy to relate to these youngsters. They were like sponges, soaking up every last bit of information I could give them; it was so exciting, we were like one big extended family.

We taught using 'chalk and talk' with information displayed on the blackboard, tables by rote and rewards for good work. There were few classroom assistants in those days so teaching was generally aimed towards the majority of the class.

The bright ones were given additional work to make sure that they thoroughly knew their subject and the less bright had one-to-one sessions with the teacher. Discipline was a word that never came into the classroom.

I was informed by one mother who pushed a reluctant child into the room one day that he 'had one on him' and was the wrong side out. She went on to inform me that if he gave me any lip I was to 'give him one behind the ear' and he would get another from his father when he came home, something I never agreed with.

I never found it necessary to reprimand any child with any physical punishment; we just used jokes and laughed at ourselves to get through. One boy in particular was the bane of my life. I did tend to shout at him and threatened that if I was made angry, I would turn into the Incredible Hulk they had seen on television. This scared them enough to always stay on my good side.

This little boy called Guy was an exception; after one incident when he was winding me up saying he didn't feel like reading today, I could feel my frustration building so altered the tone of my voice, after which he said, 'You're not going to get angry with me are you Miss? You've got lovely blue eyes.' I just melted and he complied with my wishes much better after that.

Another boy would always be humming the theme of the A Team very loudly when he stood in the reading line. He used to do my head in, so years later when he was a local pub landlord, I went to visit him. I sat on a bar stool and hummed that theme tune again. It was only then he realised how infuriating he had been and apologised.

Another boy in my class lived at the lighthouse down by the beach. It was active most of the time droning out signals from its foghorn. This led to my pupil suffering from a serious case of lack of sleep; in the few hours he did manage to get he dreamt mostly of dinosaurs. This came to fruition in the classroom where he became an expert on this subject.

When I started teaching at Pendeen in 1976, it was rather a poor area of the South-West. Gone were the affluent days of mining in this part of Cornwall, although the Geevor Tin Mine was still active and working. In fact most of the children in my class had fathers working down the mine, so the day the emergency siren droned out across the village we all went cold.

It was one of those situations where the hairs on the back of your neck stand up as I looked around my class in slow motion as each child, as one, had one thought... 'Where's dad?'

It was that quiet time after dinner which we devoted to quiet reading, so we just continued as normal, pricking up our ears as the noise, went on and on, until the inevitable question was brought up: 'What do you think is going on Miss?

With images of the Aberfan disaster coming to the front of my mind, I told the children the honest truth that I didn't know what was happening. As soon as a break came in the school day the secretary provided us with all the necessary details. Apparently there had been a fault with the cage that transported the miners to the various levels; this had broken and some men had tumbled out, but help was at hand and all were rescued which gave us all a happy ending. But it was still a fearful time for us until the all-clear was given. We had to live with this fear constantly.

In 1980 the Queen visited the mine. She went many thousands of feet underground and the workers went to great pains to whitewash the level she went down to: a great source of amusement at the time.

That day I was wearing two hats: I was the Brown Owl for the 1st Pendeen Brownies which I had established and I had to be with my class as well.

It was a bitterly cold day and the wind blew fiercely off the sea just below us, but we were informed that the Brownies had to stay in their uniforms and were not to wear their coats as they eagerly flew their flags.

So as soon as we heard the shouts saying she was coming all the coats were taken off and sometimes put on again and again, as in the excitement, there were many shouts that were false alarms; many posh cars came with leading dignitaries in them and the Queen was a long way behind

Anyway we all had a commemorative mug and medal to remind us of that splendid but very cold day all those years ago.

I also established a thriving guitar group at the school and fitted this activity in the dinner hour. On one occasion a fellow teacher came into our practice and demanded I break for dinner. She winked at the kids and said, 'I think Miss L should have a break don't you?'

She then winked at me, saying, 'Even prisoners have time off to eat you know.'

I loved this part of teaching and they learnt many songs for assembly and Cornish folk songs which were popular at the time. I used to sing a variety of these in the local pub during the summer months to entertain the trippers and can guess that many a foreigner to our region can now sing, 'Way Down To Lamorna' and 'Going up Camborne Hill coming down', in a very expert manner from that time.

Life from this time was exhausting but enjoyable; even as I started married life soon after I found it easy to take these responsibilities on board.

However when I decided to start my own family in the eighties my priorities changed somewhat and I felt that my children should come first in my life. This decision was taken from me however when in 1985 on the birth of my second child I suffered a massive stroke and the door on my teaching and singing career shut fast. I was 32.

Chapter Twelve
A MIGRAINE STROKE WHILE ON DUTY

It had begun in class one Friday afternoon. I had literally just turned around from the blackboard when stars started floating in front of my eyes; my head turned but my eyes were fixed in the last position, in a matter of seconds I felt the symptoms of a migraine coming on, the side of my face, my ear, my nose, tongue and teeth went numb.

I knew that time was precious so I hurriedly told a pupil to fetch the teacher next door. When he came in I explained that in a few minutes I would be unable to talk properly so he instantly took over and sent me to the staff room.

At this stage I just thought it was another bad headache, but this was getting more and more unpleasant as time passed. My mouth now felt as if a dentist had given me an overdose of anaesthetic, my teeth felt as if they weighed a tonne and my tongue seemed as if it had swelled to twice its size and was physically blocking my panicking words that boiled inside me.

Reaching the staff room seem to take forever. Once inside, another staff member came to my aid with aspirin and a glass of water, but as I tried to take hold of it, it just slipped from my hand and dropped to the floor spilling the water all over me. I could not concentrate on doing two things at the same time.

The first thing you think off when something happens like this is to apologise. I found I couldn't even do that, the words just wouldn't come from my brain.

As I sat there I was trying to think of a reason why this would be happening. I knew it was my menstrual time of the month. I always got headaches at this time, but never as bad as this one. Could it be something to do with the contraceptive pill I was taking? My next thought was I had to get home and see my little girl Laura-Jo. The way I was feeling I needed to see mum to ask her to take care of her, while I tried to get better by going to bed.

I felt as though I was drunk; my words were slurred and the movements had considerably slowed down. I hoped some sleep might solve the problem. When I awoke later I still had a headache and every step I took down the stairs vibrated throughout my body, ending in a loud thud in my head. Ordinary noises around me seemed amplified ten fold and I still felt like as if I was suffering from an immense hangover, but still I took more pills. Again attempting to turn on the tap and hold a glass under it proved impossible; it seemed as though I was incapable of doing two things at a time so I ended up placing the glass in the sink and filling it up that way and then I had to hold it with two hands to get it to my mouth. Dribbling just like a baby I tried and tried to drink the water. My lips were numb. I hobbled back to bed pulling myself up the stair rail with both hands till I got upstairs; then attempted to phone my sister-in-law to come over.

She hadn't been able to understand me over the phone but knew who it was by dialling 147, and came over straight away. As soon as she saw what state I was in, she phoned for an ambulance and reassured me that Laura-Jo would be okay.

Coming to Terms with the Stroke situation and Accepting I was not Dying

When I arrived at the central hospital for Cornwall which was a road journey of over two hours from where I lived, there was a medical team on standby to deal with me. I had an immediate brain scan that revealed I had had a bleed in the brain.

As this was on the right-hand side of the brain it affected the movement on the left-hand side of the body. One exercise that a doctor primarily did was to see if I could touch my nose with my left-hand finger.

How easy, I thought but I was miles out.

There must be something wrong with my eyes, I thought, but I couldn't help wondering how really stupid I had become and helpless to do anything about it.

They scratched the sole of my left foot with something sharp, nothing. What a state to be in and me an intellectual person, or so I thought.

The first thing I became aware of was being dressed up like a Michelin man with my left arm and leg inflated inside balloon-type contraptions to aid circulation.

I felt light all over, as if I was floating off somewhere, and existed in a lazy dream world for some time.

It was much later that I realised that the stroke had affected the left-hand side of my body, which, if there was any consolation from this, meant that I could still communicate easily with those around me.

It could have been so much worse, a substantial haemorrhage that could have wiped my life out in a moment or left me as a vegetable.

Yet I still felt useless and good for nothing. Although I was given the best possible treatment in intensive care and was soon able to return to the ward. When the Michelin Man accessories were removed from the affected arm I went into a kind of spastic spasm, the fingers on my hand curled together in a tight unrelenting ball and my arm recoiled defensively to settle in an iron tight grip on my chest.

Straight away I saw the physiotherapist who gently eased the arm from the chest. They explained that this had to be a slow, drawn-out procedure to coax my arm and hand into working again. The treatment hurt so badly all my arm wanted to do was to lie protectively across my chest and never think about working again.

For my part I lapsed into a state of denial that I even had a left side to my body, which was quite common I was told to stroke patients. This was overcome in part by the nurses deliberately attending to me on the affected side.

Everything that I did was heroically carried out away from the dominating right side of my body. The time soon came to access the movement in my left leg. As I was helped out of bed my left side crumbled away from me. All I was aware of was that I had a perfectly normal right-hand side to my body and I could live using just this.

As well as the leg's refusal to support me, any messages sent by my brain down my left-hand side refused to connect with each other somewhere along the line. I progressed from using a walking frame to shuffling along using a crutch and dragging the leg.

I worked on the parallel bars on the even surface. After being helped to get to them and helped back again, I had to learn to walk all over again and my thoughts went back to the various younger children I'd taught over the years who, for one reason and another, found simple tasks hard.

All I had to do, I told myself, was to place one foot in front of the other and make some progress. How hard could that be? But in reality it was near impossible for me to do. The same with my hand. Sheer determination was followed with rising frustration about not being able to perform simple acts such as spreading the fingers and keeping the hand open.

When having physiotherapy I used my right hand to demonstrate to the left one the way it should be done, but nothing happened. Touching the tip of each finger for example, with the thumb was an impossible task. Yet it was so easy for the right hand.

One day the staff of my school trooped in. Six staff and the headmaster seeing me in my nightdress and without make up: how embarrassing!

'Come back to school soon, we have no one to take your guitar group,' they pleaded.

If only I could. I was unable to walk and unfold my fingers, talk about tuning the 20 guitars in my thriving guitar group. I knew where I would have liked to be. If only I could have been in my own classroom, looking out of the window over the blue bay and watching the passing ships with my chattering, irritating seven-year-olds, that would have been bliss. It all seemed an impossible world away now

My Guitar Group, 1976-82

Conquering my Disability using one hand and Positive Thinking

There are definitely some things in life that need two hands to work... Think about it!

From the rather simple act of fastening such things as your bra, buttons and shoe laces to mention just a few, to more intimate actions such as making love. I could hold on to my partner for kissing and caressing, but I couldn't let go. Honestly it brings tears to my eyes even now, just thinking how we both tried to lead a normal sexual relationship.

What I had to do was to begin my life all over again, a clean slate. I had to learn to walk again, have years of physiotherapy. At the time I recall saying very seriously that if the stroke didn't end my life, then the therapy would. My hand and arm ached like toothache; they were pulled, pushed, cajoled and subjected to torture by ice, electric shocks and stretching but all to no avail.

Just when I thought that things could certainly not get any worse I was presented with yet another shock, when a nurse approached my bed with the results of my urine test.

'By the way Mrs A, did you know that you are pregnant?'

'What! That's impossible, I'm on the pill,' I gasped.

'Well your test shows you are about ten weeks.'

The next thing was that I was covered in lead sheeting to go for a CAT scan. The baby now was the priority in all things.

Another emergency happened shortly after when I noticed that I was bleeding, which sent the whole ward into a flurry of activity. I was given strict instructions that not under any circumstances was I allowed to get out of bed, so a boring period of bed rest ensued.

When the consultant came to assess me, he said my progress had been exceptional and he wished he had recorded my swift improvement, as this could have been used as an example to others.

He compared my stroke in the simplest terms possible to a tap being suddenly switched off in the brain and stopping the blood flow, but, he said because I was so young, the blood had found a different route to travel and he thought there would be no further restrictions to my movement than what I was dealing with at the moment.

Great!

I didn't feel as if I'd made any sort of advancement and was particularly depressed about the idea of bringing up a new baby on my own using just one hand and having no help.

As I lay there, I began to think about the tasks ahead of me, like putting on nappies. We were still in the era of using towelling nappies that had to have a liner placed in them, and all held together with a huge nappy pin. When I asked the consultant how I might do this, he replied, 'Try holding the baby down with your foot dear, you'll manage!' Typical men, I thought.

It was October and the two months to Christmas soon passed. Wards were being cleared over the holidays and it was rumoured that I might be allowed to go home for a few days.

I was missing being in school during this exciting period; as well as preparing all the singing, there was the dealing with the guitar group and the craft and parties to think about.

The next thing I thought I could do, seeing as it was impossible for me to be there, was to write cards to my class. I had cards brought in for me and I did manage to assemble two piles: one of cards and one of envelopes. Of course there was the task of opening them to write in them; as these were new and springy it was difficult but somehow I persevered and found a way of securing the card with my elbow.

But then I had to get the cards into their envelopes. This was impossible. I found I couldn't align the card to go in. Cards ended up being squashed and ripped in the process and I was getting more and more frustrated with myself at not being able to do this simple thing.

In the end cards, envelopes, pens and anything else nearby were swept angrily onto the floor and I was left in a sobbing heap till a nurse came along and put the matter right. In fact I owe my recovery to her.

In her kind gentle words she sympathised with me telling me, 'Yes, you have been through a lot, and you have a good cry and feel sorry for yourself, but remember you only have to look around this ward to see someone worse off than you.

'Look over there, there's a young lad who was in a car accident, his face is a mess, the doctors have to give him a new one, using just photographs his young wife brings in, but even worse than that his optic nerve was severed in the crash so he will be blinded for life and there's no cure.'

The nurse's words made me feel so selfish I broke down and cried some more. I was so wrapped up in my own self-pity, I didn't think about the patients around me.

Still the huge frustration simmered just under the surface. I thought about my life before all of this. I yearned so much for those times again. Why couldn't I hold a knife and fork? Open up my fingers? Wave? Play my guitar which I got so much pleasure from? I ached with the pain that it was all gone.

They say time is a healer, well maybe it is, because eventually the idea that I was a stroke SURVIVOR overcame the concept that I had been a stroke VICTIM and my life continued.

I was told that I might go home for two days over Christmas and again positive thoughts and ideas clouded my mind: Christmas dinner, presents and my own bed.

On seeing my own house and the neighbours waiting to welcome me home I wept tears of joy.

I stood on the path that led to my front door. I gave instructions to leave the wheelchair by the gate. I wanted to walk down my path on my own. This I did, but was exhausted by the time I got inside.

I must have been getting better after this because I hated and resented all the fuss everyone was making around me; I wanted to take control and be my own boss. Of course this was impossible, so I had to sit tight and just watch.

At least I was looking forward to being in my own bed, but when the time came I couldn't make it up the stairs to my own bed, so had to make do with one downstairs, so things weren't quite back to normal yet. Luckily there was a loo downstairs so that helped, but my ideas of an idyllic weekend at home didn't quite materialise.

Christmas Day arrived but more problems materialised. It started off well with the turkey cooking nicely and all was under control. But then, as we sat waiting, suddenly there was a huge blast that came from the kitchen: the cooker had exploded and the electric had gone.

Next door's was fine so dinner was saved, the turkey was passed over the fence and Christmas dinner came together and was enjoyed by all.

My partner and I thought we might get married before the birth of the baby and even thought at one stage to hold this in hospital.

As we entered 1986 I got stronger and eventually left hospital quite well. Although I had a lot of weakness down the left side and my hand was still clamped to my side, I was fine for a wedding in March of that year.

My beautiful son was born in July. When it came to giving birth I had to have a caesarean because I wasn't allowed to push and my blood pressure was very low.

It was a happy event as the baby was fine and so was I, but I knew it wasn't going to be easy to take care of my baby boy. Straight away I found it hard to hold him for feeding as again I would squeeze him too hard in the process, so some variations on the theme of this had to be devised.

I had now married the baby's father, as this seemed the right thing to do, but unfortunately had only embarked on yet another disastrous relationship.

As my baby grew, my health improved and I somehow got stronger. I was still having physiotherapy and was also in a rehabilitation programme to be assessed for driving an automatic. All my reflexes were sharp again and soon I was declared fit enough to drive.

The independence this gave me was incredible; I was beginning to be my own boss again. Unfortunately the marriage was rapidly going downhill so soon I found myself on my own again, but happy. In this way I have brought up my two children on my own, but my family have always been nearby to help. It has been due to their love and encouragement and my FIERCE POSITIVE THINKING that life has continued so well.

EPILOGUE

Living the Life of a SURVIVOR not a VICTIM

The main part in life is to make the best of what you have and what you've been given. Someone's who has had a stroke can spend all their time saying, 'Look at me, poor me… I can't do this… can't do that like I used too…' What boring people they must be to society.

Surely it's better in life to say… I can't do that the way I used to, but instead this is how I CAN do it now. Nobody really cares about your plight if you're wallowing in self-pity all day.

That's not the way to go on. Yes, I wish that I didn't have a devastating stroke at 32 that robbed me of my middle years; and wish that I was still in my classroom overlooking the sea with the challenge of teaching difficult kids. Some of my college friends are still in the same school as they were in years ago. I really wish I could play guitar; that my fingers would uncurl just that little bit so I could play the chords that are still stored in my brain.

Luckily for me my singing voice did come back. I have even had jobs in school and instead of using the guitar as my confidence provider I now use my voice.

Life after a stroke is all about Adapting

The frustration will always be there, but other doors will open if you keep an open mind. There as been a lot of water under the bridge since then; as in evolution we must adapt or become extinct like the dinosaurs.

Sunshine from the Shadows

There has been great sadness; losing dad so suddenly, and then my best friend, Lynn Laity, whom I had grown up with dying in an awful car accident, together with her husband only two years ago.

Yet there have also been many good things: my two children have grown up into lovely adults. They both have good jobs and are level-headed and independent.

So life has come round full circle; we look forward and are forward-looking to the future and life speeds on regardless.

So I leave anyone who feels they are being hammered down by life to remember something I heard on *Strictly Come Dancing* recently. They said:

'Winners never quit and

Quitters never win.'

Sunshine from the Shadows

With the dawn of a new millennium Julia set herself yet another challenge. As her children were taking exams – Laura was at last studying for a degree – after putting off going to College like the rest of her year group because she thought she should stay at home to look after her mum, Julia enrolled on a full time degree course in English; in which she joked she could 'sit around doing some serious reading without having to make excuses for it!.

She was proud to gain a B.A. 2:2 in English (Hons) at the same time Laura got a B.Ss in Social Sciences, and Perryn gained his G.C.S.E's.

This was at a ceremony where Pen Haddow (local Westcountry resident and now well-known Arctic Explorer) quoted that,

"You haven't failed at anything until you ACTUALLY give up on it!"

Julia went on to study for a P.G.C.E (Post Graduate Certificate in Education) and for a time taught adults with learning difficulties, whom she said, she had a special empathy with.

She now lives a mile from her beloved village of Perranuthoe, in the village of Goldsithney; together with her son Perryn, who is now a strapping 24year old who plays football for his local team, Mousehole F.C.